CATHOLICS COME HOME

God's Extraordinary Plan for Your Life

TOM PETERSON

Foreword by Dr. Scott W. Hahn

IMAGE

New York

Published in the United States by Image, an imprint of the Crown
Publishing Group, a division of Random House, Inc., New York.
www.crownpublishing.com

Library of Congress Cataloging-in-Publication Data
is available upon request

ISBN 978-0-385-34717-4
eISBN 978-0-385-34718-1

Printed in the United States of America

Book design: Lauren Dong
Cover design: Holly Jonas
Cover photograph: Courtesy of Catholics Come Home

10 9 8 7 6 5 4 3 2 1

First Edition

Dedicated to my beloved wife, Tricia, and our incredible
daughters, Katie, Kimberly, and Tina

CATHOLICS
COME HOME

God loves you!

Contents

Foreword

by Dr. Scott W. Hahn

We are in the midst of a New Evangelization, and I believe this book is a signal moment in its success. This book is a grace from God. It is also a sign that will lead many folks back home to the family of God, which is the Catholic Church.

Perhaps it would be good to explain what is meant by the New Evangelization. After all, Catholics have been hearing about it for the last few decades. During the pontificate of Blessed John Paul II, we heard of it often. It was something he *saw* very clearly, as if on the horizon. It's a destination toward which he patiently moved us. Way back in 1979, near the beginning of his reign as pope, he mentioned it in passing when he spoke at Nowa Huta, Poland, which was then a communist "worker's paradise" and is now a Christian pilgrimage destination (because John Paul preached there). In 1983 he spoke of the New Evangelization for the first time in a focused, intentional way, and it was already programmatic. It defined a vision. He said,

while speaking to the bishops of Latin America, that the New Evangelization was to be officially launched in 1992, because that would mark the five hundredth anniversary of the founding and first evangelizing of the Americas.

Think about it: in 1492 the three most populous Catholic countries were Spain, Italy, and France. Fast-forward five hundred years, and the three most populous Catholic countries on earth today are Brazil, Mexico, and the United States, countries that did not even exist in 1492. As Europe used to be the world's center, so now it is the Americas. And what will be in five hundred years may well depend on how we respond to the urgent call of Christ's vicars to the task of the New Evangelization. In retrospect we can see why Blessed John Paul looked back—and forward—to a *New* Evangelization that would begin in the Americas.

In preparation for that launch, he published an encyclical in 1990, *Redemptoris Missio,* and there he stated: "I sense that the moment has come to commit all of the Church's energies to a *New Evangelization.* . . . No believer in Christ, no institution of the Church, can avoid this supreme duty: to proclaim Christ to all peoples."

John Paul went on to describe the decade of the 1990s as an extended "Advent season" for the New Evangelization. In short, as Advent marks the start of

a new liturgical year, so the last decade of the twentieth century marked the beginning of the New Evangelization. This was clearly never intended to be a short-term campaign. It was a priority for Blessed John Paul from the early years of his pontificate, and he carried the New Evangelization into the new millennium. Likewise, Pope Benedict has renewed the call with even greater emphasis, and has made it clear that it is to continue for the rest of the twenty-first century!

Indeed, if some people thought of the New Evangelization as the previous pope's private catchphrase, they have by now been completely disabused of that notion. Not only has Pope Benedict taken it up with gusto, he has also specified more precisely what it means. In his teaching, he refers to two distinct "branches" of evangelization: on the one hand, "evangelization" refers to the continuous practice of the Church's missionaries who have always gone out to proclaim the Gospel to those who have never heard of Jesus Christ and his message of salvation. On the other hand, he has clarified that "the *New Evangelization* is directed principally at those who, though baptized, have drifted away from the Church and live without reference to the Christian life."

In other words, Pope Benedict is asking all of us to take up the work that Catholics Come Home® has

been doing now for years—the very task that's set before us in this book. Yes, we need to reach those millions who have never heard of Christ, but first and foremost we need to dedicate ourselves to evangelizing the baptized—to reaching those prodigal sons and daughters who have strayed from the Church. They're outside the Church looking at its stained-glass windows, which look pretty drab from the street. But if we get these people to come back inside, they'll see—and remember—the glorious, luminous beauty when the light shines in from above.

The Church "exists," said Pope Paul VI, "in order to evangelize." It is the work not just of foreign missionaries, but of the whole Church. *Evangelization* is what we do—*because we're Christian, because we're Catholic.* More than that, it's who we are. If we don't evangelize, we simply *do not exist* as Christians. Isn't it tragic that we can speak today of so many "formerly Christian" lands, in the Middle East, in Europe . . . in the Americas?

We will be patient, as the popes have been, but we must not be slack. We must feel the urgency of the sacred authors who cried out "How long?" (see Psalm 6:3) even as they knew that their Redeemer lives (see Job 19:25) and that everything would work together for the good (see Romans 8:28).

Pope Benedict clarified our mission. He stated very

frankly that we need to re-evangelize countries that have been de-Christianized, beginning with our own. It is sad that we can speak of many once-Christian lands that have drifted from their former ardor. And what America becomes largely depends on what Americans do for the New Evangelization. This is the work God has created us to do. It is work that can give greater meaning not only to the lives of those who help, but to our own as well.

I have known Tom Peterson for many years and have seen God's work in his life and in his work—Catholics Come Home, an international media evangelization apostolate like no other—and now in this exciting book. As I have said to him more than once, echoing the words of Mordecai to Esther, "Perhaps you have come to the kingdom for such a time as this?" (Esther 4:14). And, dear reader, that's true not just for Tom, but also for you.

Our family is made up of every race.
We are young and old, men and women, sinners and saints.
Our family has spanned the centuries and the globe.
With God's grace, we started hospitals to care for the sick.
We establish orphanages and help the poor.

We are the largest charitable organization on the planet, bringing
relief and comfort to those in need.
We educate more children than any other scholarly or religious
institution.
We developed the scientific method and laws of evidence.
We founded the college system.

We defend the dignity of all human life and uphold marriage and
family.
Cities were named after our revered saints, who navigated a sacred
path before us.
Guided by the Holy Spirit, we compiled the Bible.

We are transformed by sacred Scripture and sacred Tradition,
which have consistently guided us for two thousand years.
We are the Catholic Church,
with over one billion in our family
sharing in the sacraments and fullness of Christian faith.
For centuries we have prayed for you and our world,
every hour of every day, whenever we celebrate the Mass.

*Jesus, Himself, laid the foundation for our faith when He said to
    Peter, the first pope,*
"You are rock, and upon this rock I will build My Church."
*For over two thousand years we have had an unbroken line of
    shepherds*
*guiding the Catholic Church with love and truth in a confused and
    hurting world.*

And in this world, filled with chaos, hardship, and pain,
*it's comforting to know that some things remain consistent, true,
    and strong—*
*our Catholic faith, and the eternal love that God has for all
    creation.*

*If you've been away from the Catholic Church, we invite you to
    take another look.*
Ours is one family united in Jesus Christ, our Lord and Savior.
We are Catholic. Welcome home.

God's Extraordinary Plan for You

*Few souls understand what God would accomplish in them
if they were to abandon themselves unreservedly to Him and
if they were to allow His grace to mold them accordingly.*

SAINT IGNATIUS OF LOYOLA

God has something extraordinary planned for your
life.

Let me say that again slowly because it's really important.

> God
>> has
>>> something
>>>> extraordinary
>>>>> planned
>>>>>> for
>>>>>>> your
>>>>>>>> life!

In our fast-paced, highly technological world, this statement might sound a bit lofty, but the lives of millions of souls who have come before us attest to this simple truth:

God has a wonderful plan in store for *you*.

God wants you to be happy. He wants you to experience His unfailing compassion. He wants you to feel the warmth of mercy and to share His love with others. God wants you to know that you exist for a reason. Discovering God's plan for your life is rather easy, yet, to be honest, somewhat difficult, too. It starts with saying yes to the Holy Spirit and allowing Him to guide you. Living a God-affirming life is ultimately a decision that each of us needs to make. Sometimes it can be a tough decision. Does saying yes to God mean saying no to the secular world? To an extent it does, but let me tell you, the exchange rate is in your favor when you trade in your old life for a new life in Christ! The chaos, noise, and distractions of secular society lure millions of souls away from God. But it doesn't have to be that way. There are heroic role models who exist or have existed in the din of all this craziness, yet have still lived deeply spiritual lives. In fact, their heroic mission in life was to make the lives of those around them more, well, humane.

Let's look at Mother Teresa as one such heroic ex-

ample. Mother thrived spiritually even in the squalor and uncertainty of a country where thousands died from malnutrition and hardship every day! She took what some would call the throwaways of life, people few thought of as human, and helped them to regain their human dignity. With trustful surrender to God's Divine providence, Mother Teresa left the security of the Loreto Sisters convent in India with five rupees and wearing a sari to accept a life of poverty, living among the poorest Indians. She took up her mission in the slums of Calcutta not knowing where she would make a home or how she would survive. She put total trust in God that since He gave her the mission, He would take care of her. Interestingly, as recent books have indicated, even Mother Teresa struggled with her faith. But you know what? She knew her purpose in life and trusted the Holy Spirit to lead the way. This isn't to say she didn't have moments when she may have struggled or doubted, yet she consistently maintained a clear vision of what she had to do: love and serve God and others. Each of us, not just Mother Teresa, is also called to love and serve. It is God's will for His children.

YOU CAN BECOME A HERO OF
THE FAITH

Mother Teresa, granted, is an extreme example of sacrificial love and service in a vocational calling. You probably know more people *unlike* her than you do people *like* her. You probably know people who are indifferent to the spiritual life, who have generally forgotten God and devoted themselves entirely to the pursuit of what they believe to be success and happiness. This is why I wrote this book—to share with you and the people around you proven ways to enter into a deeper relationship with God and His Church, and to help bring your relatives and neighbors home to our universal Catholic family as well.

The fundamental core mission of this book is to help you become a lay witness of the New Evangelization. What does this mean? Being a lay witness of the New Evangelization is about breaking out of your nine-to-five routine in order to live a more heroic Catholic life, a destiny designed not just for priests and nuns, nor intended just for deacons and monks, but for you and me, the ordinary folks in the pews. We must be witnesses who attest to the wonders of being in a covenant relationship with the resurrected Christ, and

who live as active members of His family, the Holy Catholic Church. By learning and sharing your Catholic faith, you too can experience the greatest adventure of your life as you give yourself more completely, more passionately, to the will of God and the promptings of the Holy Spirit. It all boils down to doing one thing: surrendering yourself to Divine Providence, trusting that God will provide you with everything you need.

In order to begin on this path, first learn your faith; after all, you cannot give what you do not have. The Most Reverend David L. Ricken, chairman of the U.S. Conference of Catholic Bishops Committee on Evangelization and Catechesis, said, "In order to evangelize, a person must first be evangelized. This is really at the heart of the New Evangelization."

There is more: You must be receptive to being filled with Christ's mercy, grace, and love. Once you are immersed in the love of Christ, you can better share His love with others.

The time for us to act is now, since the world keeps moving faster, and more and more of our loved ones are being drawn away from the Catholic faith. Many drift away from God altogether. Atheism and agnosticism are growing at alarming rates. The Church and the world are in dire need of true Christian witnesses,

authentic and dedicated heroes of the faith, modern-day saints who will help lead more souls to heaven. *You* have been called to be one of these hero-saints!

Leon Bloy, a French novelist and fervent convert to Catholicism, once wrote, "There is only one tragedy in the end . . . not to have been a saint." Our Lord's greatest desire for you is to become a saint, to be holy. In 2 Timothy 1:9 Saint Paul says, "[God] saved us and called us with a holy calling, not in virtue of our works but in virtue of his own purpose and the grace which he gave us in Christ Jesus ages ago."

WHY ME? WHY NOW?

Columbia magazine, a monthly publication published by my brother Knights of the Knights of Columbus, reported that Pope Benedict XVI said: "The greatest crisis facing our world is the absence of God. We all need God." Our mission, as the body of Christ, is to spread the good news of Jesus to the world.

The need for Christian love in our society is real, and it is serious. Our world is starving for the spiritual. At baptism, the Holy Spirit placed in each of us a type of homing device, a kind of GPS—*a God Positioning System*—to help us find our way back to God, home

to His Church. But many people have unplugged their GPS from its power source, by abandoning the Mass and the sacraments. Only one of every four Catholics currently practices their faith regularly and attends weekly Mass. Consequently, many have lost their way and don't know the route back. We need to help these wandering Catholics and others to find their way home.

Since 1965, weekly Mass attendance has plummeted from 71 percent at its peak to a meager 17 percent in 2008. This pandemic hits home for every faithful practicing Catholic, since we all have very close family members and friends who have drifted away from the sacraments, the Catholic Church, and even from God Himself. We miss these loved ones, we pray for them, and we are deeply concerned for their salvation, as we should be.

While roughly 24 percent of Americans are baptized Catholics, statistics from the Pew Research Center show that only one out of four baptized Catholics practices their faith regularly by going to Sunday Mass. A large percentage never go to Mass, and some may go infrequently, perhaps at Christmas or Easter. So when you study these sobering statistics, you realize that only 6 percent of Americans are practicing Catholics. According to Georgetown University's Center for the

Study of Global Christianity, the statistics for Europe are even worse, with churches virtually empty in many countries.

Barna Group research shows that there has been a 92 percent increase in the number of unchurched Americans since 1991. Indifference is escalating, and more people justify being lukewarm in their faith, since so many other people are doing much worse things. Another epidemic is *moral relativism,* whose adherents point out that people disagree on what is moral, and therefore there is no objective right or wrong, and since no one is right or wrong, they advocate that we should tolerate others' behavior even if we don't agree with it. Another growing philosophy is *secular humanism,* whose proponents believe that human beings are capable of being ethical and moral without religion or a god. Secularism is growing across the world, where souls are falling for the distractions and materialism of this world and giving them priority over God and His teachings. Last but not least, we see *agnosticism* and *atheism* growing exponentially.

WE CAN'T SHARE WHAT WE DON'T HAVE

Before we can be fruitful in leading people home to Jesus and His Church, we need to grow closer to God ourselves. This is where my spiritual journey and personal story come into play. For most of my life I was a perfunctory Catholic. Sure, I went to Sunday Mass, prayed, and fasted and abstained on the days prescribed by the Church. But for me, these were routines for the most part. What was truly important to me were my family, my career, my friends, my goals. Don't get me wrong, family, work, friends, and goals are all important, and we displease God if we neglect them. Yet Jesus instructs us that the greatest commandment is this: "You shall love the Lord your God with all your heart, and with all your soul, and with all your mind, and with all your strength" (Mark 12:30). But that is not how I loved God. He existed on the periphery of my life; I barely thought of Him unless I needed something. Those days are over, and part of this book tells the story of how God brought me back into full communion with the Church and transformed my life. My hope is that my story may help you discover God's plan for your life and, God willing, open an exciting new

door for you, one that brings you and those around you deeper into the faith.

Since I accepted God's invitation to receive His love and mercy, my life was been blessed with a deep purpose and happiness I had never felt before. While my heart experienced a profound conversion, essentially my soul was undergoing a "reversion" home to my Catholic roots, the sacramental graces I received at my baptism, my first confession, my first Holy Communion, and my confirmation. The sacramental graces never left me, but the flame of my spiritual pilot light needed to be fanned by the breath of the Holy Spirit. Maybe yours does, too?

CATHOLICS COME HOME . . . LOTS OF THEM!

Not long after my awakening of faith, the epiphany that led to my reversion, I discovered that God was also calling me to help others on their journey home. With God's grace, I established an international media evangelization apostolate called Catholics Come Home. Little did I know that in just three years over 125 million viewers would see our new and inspiring television commercials and visit our bilingual websites. And after seeing these evangelization ads we call *evangomercials*™

more than 350,000 people would come home to Jesus and His Church!

Why has Catholics Come Home been so effective and attracted so much international attention? Catholics Come Home works because it provides a simple invitation to people, meets them where they are, and gives them an easy way to begin their journey home to Jesus and His Church. I believe that deep down, most people really want to be better and do more good in the world. Many people want to grow closer to God, to trust in him, but they just don't know where to begin. We've witnessed that many of these regular folks begin their journey back to Jesus and the Church after seeing an inviting television message during their favorite program. When they've been asked, "Why did you come home?" the vast majority answer, "Because you invited me!" This is how Catholics Come Home is answering the call of the New Evangelization. Each of us is called by God to spread His good news and bring souls home as well. After all, this is our prime mission as members of the Church, and our duty as baptized Christians.

As an added outreach to their local Catholics Come Home campaigns, some lay Catholics have formed door-to-door prayer teams. When they've gone around their neighborhoods, they've said, for example, "I'm

from St. Anne's Catholic parish, and a number of us will be praying at church in front of the Blessed Sacrament for the needs of families in our neighborhood. How can we pray for you and your family?" We've heard stories of people who have been brought to tears because someone offered to pray for a spouse who lost a job, a parent with cancer, or a child with a drug addiction. Door-to-door evangelization has been a successful outreach. When Catholics are proud of their faith, understand their faith, and have a close relationship with Christ, our Church blossoms and attracts souls.

A NEW SPRINGTIME OF HOPE

Whether we share our beautiful Catholic faith by broadcasting television evangomercials inviting souls home, or we discuss our faith with relatives, neighbors, friends, or coworkers in person, the Holy Spirit often chooses to work through faithful followers, *if we are willing*. Are you willing?

When we embrace God and He embraces us back, we become filled with a passion to share the good news of Jesus with the world. After all, that is the core mission of the body of Christ. It's why the Church exists. Through our Christian baptism, you and I are commissioned to evangelize, to proclaim Jesus to the world,

and to help others discover the fullness of faith, and for Catholics that means everything that the Catholic Church has to offer.

If the thought of sharing your faith with others makes you anxious, bear with me. You do not have to quit your job or sell your home, give up your family, enter a seminary, or spend the remainder of your mortal life tucked away in a convent. While that may be the courageous path prepared for some saints, it's typically not the route God has designed for most regular people like you and me who need to live *in* the world but are reminded so beautifully in the Gospels that we are not to be *of* the world. The path to being an apostle of Christ today begins with igniting a spark of passion for your faith, then adding a bit of *heroism* to your life. It's about climbing out of the hole of lukewarm mediocrity to live a more vibrant, committed, and passionate faith. It's about finding true purpose and meaning for your life. Remember what Pope Benedict XVI wrote in 2010 in his post-synodal apostolic exhortation *Verbum Domini*: "We cannot keep to ourselves the words of eternal life given to us in our encounter with Jesus Christ: they are meant for everyone, for every man and woman. . . . It is our responsibility to pass on what, by God's grace, we ourselves have received."

—◦❦ ❦◦—

The surest route to being a more heroic Catholic today is by living God's will, trusting the Holy Spirit to guide you, using your God-given talents and interests to their fullest potential, and serving those who are struggling with faith. Ultimately these acts of heroism lead to sainthood. Again, don't be put off by a word that may have intimidating connotations. In fact, *all* baptized Christians are called to be saints. Granted, few of us will ever be formally canonized by the Church, but remember that every soul in heaven is a saint. How is that so? By the simple fact that when we go to heaven we are joined to God forever. And that is our goal—eternal salvation with all the blessed in the kingdom of heaven. Becoming a saint starts with being rooted firmly in the truths of the faith, attending Mass, frequent reception of Jesus in the Eucharist, obeying the Ten Commandments and the teachings of the Church, studying Sacred Scripture, and availing yourself of the sacrament of Reconciliation when you sin and fall short.

HOW THIS BOOK WILL HELP

Today there are so many people who are lost and broken. Helping these souls find their way back home is

not only a duty; it is an act of mercy. It means doing what you can do to bring a soul back into a state of grace. This will not require preaching on street corners or confronting notorious sinners (again, unless God is calling you to this type of work). Instead, I'm hoping this book will help demonstrate how the right word or the right action at the right time can be decisive in helping your relatives, friends, neighbors, coworkers, and even strangers find their way home. This book also suggests ways to circumvent roadblocks and overcome challenges that lie ahead of you in your apostolic mission to get to heaven and help bring as many people with you as possible. And finally, in reading through this book you will pick up some valuable tools to help you grow in happiness and fortitude, to help you cross the finish line with your eyes firmly fixed on heaven every step of the way.

If this still sounds a bit overly ambitious to you, I understand how you feel. I felt that way, too, at first. But over time, I've come to believe for myself that with God all things are indeed possible!

DETOURING OFF THE BRIDGE

Imagine that you are viewing a massive and beautiful bridge spanning a cavernous river gorge. On one side of

the bridge is a busy city filled with millions of inhabitants, tall buildings, and various noisy commercial and passenger vehicles. On the opposite side of the bridge is a lush, peaceful tropical paradise filled with fruit trees, flowers, waterfalls, streams, and quaint cottages, but relatively few people.

At some point you realize that while numerous cars are heading toward the bridge from the city, relatively few cars are actually completing their trip over to the other side. Most of the cars are actually getting off at the very last exit before the bridge. In fact, for every twenty-four cars that approach the bridge between the city and the tropical paradise, only six make their way across.

Why not just take the bridge to paradise? Well, this, believe it or not, happens every day. What do I mean? Let me explain.

The Catholic Church serves as our wonderful bridge, a solid support structure, designed by Jesus Himself, to carry us and our families across the deep and tumultuous currents of the world, guiding our journey home to heaven. Yet sadly only a small percentage of travelers are actually staying on this bridge and crossing safely to the other side. Also very few observers are volunteering to help wave the caution flags,

in an effort to help direct families safely to their ultimate destination.

It seems as if nearly all of us have friends, close relatives, neighbors, and coworkers who have veered off the Catholic bridge to try *other routes*. In fact, some have abandoned their faith journey altogether and are heading back to the apparent glitter of the big city. Still others just run out of gas, stalling before crossing over the spiritual bridge, and ending their progress at some point along the way.

Today many families in our world are driving along aimlessly. So many people are searching for God, looking for a retreat from the chaos, but they just don't know how to escape the urban din. Few souls truly understand that nothing other than God will satisfy their search for happiness.

But this is exactly why we must help, now! In fact, Jesus is calling all of His followers, to assist Him by inviting the multitudes to a better way that will eventually lead more people safely home. You and I are being called to help in this critical rescue mission for souls. And when we serve Jesus in helping these weary travelers with some needed direction, we will discover true purpose and experience real happiness in our own lives, too!

ADVENTURES WITH GOD!

At this point I'd like to briefly tell you a little bit about my life's journey, which has had its own unique path. To be honest, there was nothing all that extraordinary about my beginnings. My 1960s Midwestern Catholic middle-class upbringing was normal. In fact, it was just plain ordinary, with a stay-at-home mom and a dad who had a stable career working for the U.S. Postal Service. It was not until high school that the talents and interests that would shape my vocation started to become evident. In retrospect, I can see that God blessed me with academic abilities, public speaking skills, a logical business mind, creativity, and ambition. These gifts would prove fruitful in college, in my first marketing and advertising jobs out of college, and eventually for our Catholics Come Home apostolate.

Early in my career I met my wife, Tricia, and we married. In the years that followed our family was blessed with three incredible and beautiful daughters. At this point in my life I was just a lukewarm Catholic. My faith was not a high priority, particularly as my career began to advance. The pursuit of wealth, honor, power, and achievement took all of my waking hours, and I gave these things precedence over God. I had a sizable income, a big house, nice cars. Although these

comforts were fun for a time, the novelty always faded and I began to covet the next new toy that would bring me some excitement for another month or two.

Looking back, I realize that I nearly sold my soul, forfeiting my peace and investing every waking moment to acquire and maintain all the trappings the world tells us are important. My days became exhausting; slowly I was being enslaved by the desire for a bigger home, a nicer car, and even more personal success. My spiritual pilot light, ignited at baptism and fueled by the sacraments and a solid Catholic education, had nearly been extinguished. The sad fact was that I had no idea what was going on. It was all a slow fade into a strange, almost surreal fuzziness. Have you ever felt this way? If you have, stop for a moment and ask yourself now what secular things or material pursuits may be holding you back from realizing real happiness and a closer spiritual walk with Jesus? At some point we need to realize that these signs of success easily become false idols that replace God in our hearts. And the idols aren't free; they come at a very hefty cost.

A few of my friends from church saw that my priorities were grossly out of order, so they invited me on a men's retreat. I had been uplifted by retreats as a teenager, but because of distractions in recent years I hadn't made attending a retreat a priority. I was kind

of ambivalent about my friends' proposition. My mind was racing with responsibilities at the time, but finally I decided that at least getting away would be an opportunity to decompress a bit. Maybe I could get some rest.

But something amazing happened on this retreat. Before we continue, let's look at this word *retreat* for a moment. Certainly it means going away to pray and commune with God, but militaristically it also means "to flee," and, probably, without knowing it at the time, I needed to flee from the superficiality and chaos of my life. In a moment of pure grace, I reconnected with God. How, you might wonder? Simply put, I finally shut up and let God talk to me in the quiet of my heart, and what He told me changed my life forever. Inspired by the Holy Spirit, my family began downsizing and simplifying our lives. When I started making room for Jesus in my heart and investing my time in other people, my true calling became evident: to use the talents with which God had blessed me for the good of the Church and the New Evangelization.

Within a few months after my reversion experience on that retreat, by the grace of God, two new media apostolates were born: VirtueMedia™, dedicated to promoting the pro-life cause and Catholics Come Home, dedicated to advancing the New Evan-

gelization called for first by Pope John Paul II and more recently by Pope Benedict XVI. To some, the glamour and fast-paced world of television production may sound exciting and impressive, but, honestly, both apostolates had humble beginnings. VirtueMedia began in our spare bedroom as a part-time effort financed for the first few years by my day job. We started by creating two pro-life ads: one to help pregnant women who were abortion-vulnerable, the second to offer hope and healing to women who have had an abortion. Honestly, I knew relatively little about unplanned pregnancies and even less about postabortion healing. But it seemed God was calling me to use my advertising background to help promote the sanctity of life to society, and to encourage women facing unplanned pregnancies to choose motherhood or adoption for their unborn babies. So I learned what I could, and I learned fast.

VirtueMedia aired its first commercials on local Phoenix area television stations. We had no idea what the response would be—or even if we would get a response. About eight months after the first ad ran, I held a newborn baby, Baby Jerry, in my arms. Our commercials offer a toll-free number *866-88-Woman* and a link to our informational website *PregnancyLine.org*, both of which connect pregnant women with a choice

of local pregnancy centers in their area. These commercials provided the information and resources necessary to convince Baby Jerry's mother not to have an abortion. Next came Baby Ashlynn, and then many others, thanks be to God.

Over time, as VirtueMedia's pro-life ads began airing regionally, nationally, and internationally, the lives of many more babies were saved. To our astonishment, when the ads aired nationally on MTV and BET, within one month approximately 22,000 pregnant women responded, asking for help. While we were thrilled by the incredible response to the ads, we were overwhelmed by the realization that so many pregnant women had been considering ending the lives of their babies. It was a reminder to us of the terrible toll of abortion on demand in this country; over 54 million babies have been aborted since 1973. But all those phone calls from all of those pregnant women were also evidence of God's mercy at work in the world.

Over the years I've had the privilege of meeting and developing close friendships with prominent leaders of the pro-life movement. These men and women are the heroes of our day. One in particular, the Most Reverend Thomas J. Olmsted, Bishop of Phoenix, taught me that *"it's hard to form people in virtue, if they are not first formed in faith."* Bishop Olmsted's wise observation inspired

the growth of Catholics Come Home, founded in 1997. Nearly a decade prior, Pope John Paul II published *Christifideles Laici*, a post-synodal apostolic exhortation in which he urged the lay faithful to participate fully in their vocation to bring the message of Jesus Christ to the world, especially through the modern media. Catholics Come Home was our answer to the Holy Father's call. We did not begin with a formal marketing plan, but we were filled with enthusiasm about bringing our Catholic faith to the widest possible audience. Our ads spotlight the history, beauty, spirituality, and accomplishments of our Catholic Church. The evangelization commericals, which we call evangomercials, encourage viewers to seek a personal relationship with Jesus, remind them of His Divine Mercy, and teach them that Jesus came not to condemn the world but to save it! Our goal was to draw non-Catholics and inactive Catholics home to the Church.

Once again, we saw the Lord guiding us. Led by the Holy Spirit, within the first few years after Catholics Come Home ran its first messages, over 350,000 souls returned to the Catholic faith, based on reports from partner dioceses. The ads aired from Seattle to Boston, from St. Louis to New Orleans, from Corpus Christi to Sacramento. Within three years, nearly thirty-three archdioceses and dioceses had run these "come home"

invitations. In the wake of the ads, many dioceses reported notable increases in Mass attendance, averaging about 10 percent in most dioceses, rising as high as nearly 18 percent in others. When parishes asked returnees, "Why did you come home?" the vast majority answered, "Because you invited me." How incredible God is! Our contribution was modest, yet God multiplied it as once He multiplied a handful of loaves and fishes to feed thousands.

Then, on December 16, 2011, for the first time in the history of the Catholic Church in America, or of any religion for that matter, Catholics Come Home television commercials began airing on prime-time television on major networks including CBS, NBC, Univision, CNN, USA, TBS, and others. Based on Nielsen ratings, over 125 million people were being invited home, seeing the evangomercials ten times each during the campaign. The evidence of God's mercy is overwhelming. Without God we can do nothing, but with God all good things are possible! Regular people like us just need to show up with our God-given talents—our "loaves and fishes"—and join our Lord's team in this vital mission to rescue souls.

You are uniquely blessed with your own set of talents, gifts, charisms, ideas, and inspirations of the Spirit. You are called to serve God in your workplace

or school, in your neighborhood, and among your family. If you haven't done so already, now is the time to discern your vocation, to discover how God is calling you to participate in your own personal adventure of the New Evangelization to help Catholics come home.

FULFILLING YOUR HEART'S DEEPEST DESIRE

God desires to fulfill the deepest longings of your heart and make your dreams come true. He is always willing and able to help you, no matter what your strengths or shortcomings, how old or young you are, whatever your income or career, regardless of where you live. Our Father truly has a wonderful, action-packed plan and purpose for your life. He will meet you where you are, at the moment you sincerely open your heart to invite Him in. Saint Teresa of Avila tells us, "Since He does not force our will, He takes what we give Him; but He doesn't give Himself completely until we give ourselves completely."

So read on and enjoy some incredible stories of God's love and mercy, and discover a world hidden from the proud and powerful. Along the way you'll encounter

some wisdom that can help you in your daily struggles. Simplify your life, refocus your attention on Jesus, celebrate new beginnings, and RSVP to the greatest family reunion of all time. Together you and I will learn how to serve God and our neighbors more generously. When we do so, our Lord will use us to help heal our wounded culture, advance the New Evangelization, and guide lost, unhappy souls back to the safety of home.

If we let Christ into our lives, we lose nothing, nothing, absolutely nothing of what makes life free, beautiful, and great. No! Only in this friendship are the doors of life opened wide. Only in this friendship is the great potential of human existence truly revealed.

POPE BENEDICT XVI

Chapter 1

Downsize and Simplify

The greatest challenge of the day is: how to bring about a revolution of the heart, a revolution which has to start with each one of us?

DOROTHY DAY, *The Catholic Worker*

Say the word *idol* and most people think of a statue of a pagan god. That's an accurate definition, but it is not the whole story. Too many of us have idols that take the form of money, career, beauty, a big house, a fancy car, expensive vacations, and even the admiration of our peers. According to our faith, if even so much as one of these things has primacy in your life, then you are worshipping an idol.

I know what I'm talking about, because there was a time when my life had more idols than days of the week. God had a relatively small place in my heart, no priority nor real importance in my life. Yet in His mercy He touched me and called me back to Him. From that

moment I knew that my idols had to vanish, and God needed to be enthroned where He belongs—at the center of my life. But it took a while for me to come to that realization.

In the 1990s, when my career was taking off, it wasn't unusual for me to wake up at three in the morning. My mind would be racing and sleep proved elusive. With my eyes still closed, I'd make a mental list of all the tasks and responsibilities awaiting me. I put in long days, very long, tiring fourteen-hour days. I wasn't feeling much peace, and I certainly wasn't very happy. I began to think that there had to be more to life than this.

Does this sound hauntingly familiar to you or someone you know? So many of us are exhausted from trying to achieve the American dream. We want to be happy, we long for peace, we yearn to love and be loved, yet most of us have no idea how to find what it is we are longing for inside.

God wants you to be happy, truly happy. He is your loving Father who created you for greatness. God wants to reveal His love to you, and in turn He wants you to share His love with others. But there are so many obstacles that keep you and me from being truly happy. All of us are carrying heavy burdens—perhaps emotional scars from childhood, or job loss, or illness, or

family challenges, or anxiety about how to meet financial obligations. And we may be a bit disappointed with ourselves that we aren't as kind, loving, and productive as we would like to be. Is it any surprise that we ask, "Is this all there is to life?"

These days, societal pressure to be more and more competitive starts at a younger age. Young people can feel overwhelmed by the pressure to excel in sports, academics, and social settings. There are an ever-increasing number of distractions that lure them away from their Christian faith—the one area of their lives in which they can find happiness and purpose. And it only gets worse once they join the workforce.

Once again, I am speaking now from personal experience. Upon beginning my corporate career I felt invincible. I was goal-oriented but, unfortunately, also self-centered. And my arrogance increased when, fresh out of my business marketing education from Arizona State University, I was offered a highly lucrative job in marketing in which I could earn more than graduates with chemical engineering degrees. Sometime around my twenty-second birthday the debate was whether I should buy a red Ferrari or a condo. (Thankfully, reason won out and I chose the more practical condo.)

Two years later I met and married Tricia, a beautiful and kindhearted physical therapist. Tricia is the

greatest blessing of my life, as are our three spirited daughters: Katie, Kimberly, and Kristina. During the early years of our marriage my income exploded beyond the six-figure threshold, so we did what any financially well-off young family would do—we spent it. Tricia helped me design and build a custom lakefront home in a gated community outside Phoenix, Arizona. I collected classic sports cars and the latest luxury sedans. Our family and friends believed we were living the American dream, but down deep I knew something was wrong. Upon reaching the age of thirty, I had a chronic aliment some sociologists call "Affluenza," defined as "the bloated, sluggish, and unfulfilled feeling that results from efforts to keep up with the Joneses"; and "an epidemic of stress, overwork, waste and indebtedness caused by pursuit of the American dream." My compulsion to amass more and more material stuff was simply a futile attempt to fill the void in my heart.

At the same time, without realizing it, God faded even more into the background. Jesus wasn't really part of my moral compass either, and the Catholic faith wasn't a high priority in my life. I invested very little time in prayer, although, ironically, I never missed Mass on Sunday. Oh, you would see me there, but I was there mostly out of obligation and to continue the family tradition. For me at that time, putting in an hour

at Mass on Sunday was like punching a time clock at a boring job. It was a chore and a duty, but that was it. During the sixty minutes every Sunday I would usually daydream, look around to find familiar faces of friends and neighbors, wonder what was for lunch, and plan the remainder of my day. In spite of being physically present at Mass each week, my soul was absent, and my heart and mind were in another place altogether.

As I focused more and more on worldly success and achievement, the pilot light of my childhood spirituality began to flicker and dim, and the number and variety of my sins increased: pride, anger, harsh judgments of others, greed, gluttony, and so many other sins. Money was becoming my idol. I was addicted to the sense of power that security and control brought me.

As my sins became habitual, and my conscience became desensitized, I fell deeper and deeper into the abyss of moral relativism, to the point where sins didn't feel wrong anymore. I justified my actions by telling myself, "You're not as bad as a lot of people in the news. After all, you're not a criminal or one of those notorious sinners. Besides, a loving God will let you into heaven, especially if He grades the entrance exam on a curve."

Then, while on that retreat on a hot June day in 1997, God mercifully reversed the direction of my

life. Sitting during a prayer service, I began to feel a profound change come over me. In front of me the Eucharist was enthroned in a monstrance, and I was transfixed by the light that seemed to be emanating from the altar. Then my pastor, Father Doug, whom I had known for some time, and men from my parish prayed over me. Soon the spiritual floodgates opened and I was bathed in God's compassion. I became aware of my shortcomings and sins. It was as if a light had been turned on to illuminate everything, providing me with a sense of clarity I'd never experienced before. My heart felt moved—really moved—as if my soul was trying to throw off dead weight from all the materialist burdens I had accumulated over the years. It felt like the kind of blast when someone power washes the side of a house. It felt like being washed clean, as if I were experiencing my baptism all over again. Maybe I was finally understanding my baptism for the very first time. That afternoon I made a full confession and gratefully received God's forgiveness and merciful healing. This realization, this epiphany, was like a light switch being turned on. Though I would never compare myself to Saint Paul, the story of his conversion on the road to Damascus really hit home for me. I had been on the road of life and thought I was see-

ing clearly, only to learn that I'd been walking around blind. After this experience I began to see priorities in a completely different way.

The Holy Spirit was giving me another chance, a complete do-over. In fact, God gives all of us second chances, third chances, and more thanks to His unfailing Divine Mercy. That day I felt a bit like Ebenezer Scrooge after he had seen a vision of his own death and realized he was still alive and had a chance to change his life. God began teaching me with incredible kindness. It was as if He was saying, "You've got one foot in My world and one foot in the secular world. Choices are often black or white, but you're living in the gray area, mixing the two. You've been trying to have it both ways, but now you need to choose sides. Do you want to be on my team? Then follow Me, Tom. Downsize and simplify."

Downsize and simplify.

The Holy Spirit gave me the grace that made it easy to say yes, and when I accepted this direction my whole life changed for the better.

After my retreat, when I was thirty-five, my family, friends, and coworkers all witnessed my positive transformation. I began downsizing my ego and simplifying everything in my life. No longer would I drive

ninety miles an hour on the Phoenix freeways, weaving in and out of slower traffic, thinking my appointments were more important than those of other drivers. Easing off the gas pedal literally slowed down my life. By reducing my speed by thirty-five miles per hour, slowing down my dangerously fast life, not only did I save gas, but my driving more slowly also saved lives (and likely my own). No longer would I habitually drop the F-bomb or other swear words in normal conversation. Simplifying my life meant editing out all the nonsense I didn't need—and when I did this successfully, daily life was less burdensome. Soon I started to treat people with more kindness, more compassion, more honesty, more tenderness, and I became more Christ-like. Don't get me wrong, I still had my moments of failure, and still do to this day—after all, we are only human—but by the grace of God, I was a new creation. The Divine Mercy of Jesus, as well as the prayers of many faithful family members and friends, had brought about my return, my reversion to the fullness of the Catholic faith. The Holy Spirit had guided me home, and now I felt I needed to respond out of love and gratitude by helping other souls on their journey home. We show our thankfulness to God by following His commandments and doing His will. Helping others draw closer to Christ is God's will.

That retreat experience saved my soul and maybe even my life. Shortly after the retreat I met with Father Doug for spiritual direction. During our time together he taught me about an important concept he called "the double-edged sword." God has blessed each of us with unique gifts and talents, Father Doug said, and often these gifts and talents are the exact weapons the devil uses to tempt us into sin. For example, someone with the gift of physical beauty may be tempted to commit the sins of vanity, lust, and pride. (Think of the way beautiful women are portrayed in advertising and the way men respond; take my word for it, I worked in the industry and beauty isn't always pretty.) A person with the gift of eloquence may be tempted to use that gift to wound others by twisting words around or playing to other people's egos so as to manipulate them. If you've ever read Dante's classic poem *Inferno*, you know that hell is populated by many people who used words to deceive others. But for now, let's refocus on the gifts God has given to you and how you can grow in faith.

As discussed earlier in the introduction, I want this book to help you on your faith journey, so let's take a few moments to do a little spiritual survey right now! First off, let's start by saying a little prayer together.

Jesus, help me to trust in You and do Your will.

Not so tough. Just say those words and hold them inside for a few moments. When you're ready, ask yourself two questions: In what areas do I need improvement? And in what areas has God blessed me with gifts? Now, think about how you can downsize and simplify your life and improve upon your weaknesses. For instance, maybe you're impatient. What can you do to downsize that impatience? What can you do to simplify the way you respond to complex situations? Essentially, ask yourself, What can I live *without* in my life? Maybe you drop four-letter words, or you scream or talk loudly. Maybe you worry too much, when deep down you know that God will provide, and you just can't seem to let go of the anxiety or the need to be in control of *everything*. Aren't you carrying around a bunch of extra baggage in your life? It's almost as if we're Christmas trees that are adorned with too many gaudy ornaments, added weight and clutter we just don't need and can't support. Here we are alive and doing our work when something happens. Rather than going to Jesus, the Prince of Peace, for help, we respond to life's challenges in a warped, inferior way that makes our lives even more burdensome. So we begin to adorn ourselves with a few heavy balls of tension, and then a few rows of electrified words, then string along a few

boxes of tinseled yelling. What do we have? Well, a pretty sad, ugly, and chaotic-looking Christmas tree.

Downsize and simplify.

Meditate on these words of Blessed John Paul II: "It is necessary to awaken again in believers a full relationship with Christ. . . . Only from a personal relationship with Jesus can an effective evangelization develop."

Now, a few more words. Do not make the mistake of thinking that it is all up to you to bring about changes in yourself and others. We all need help. And that help is found only in the Blessed Trinity and in the teachings of the Church. There are so many opportunities for us to learn from those who have come before us. Who better to teach us than Jesus and His family of saints, our cousins in the Catholic faith. So ask for their help. Pray that prayer:

Jesus, help me to trust in You and do Your will.

Remember, ultimately it is our Heavenly Father, Jesus, and the Holy Spirit who convert hearts, *not* you and me. So pray to the Holy Spirit for guidance. Ask for His direction on how you can best use your gifts and talents to help others to come home, and for wisdom to downsize and simplify all areas of your life that

keep you from growing in faith. Always remember that it is God and His holy angels who do the heavy lifting. And that's a good thing. Have you ever seen the wings on Saint Michael? He's got to have some strong back muscles to keep those massive wings in the air!

For God is at work in you, both to will and to work for his good pleasure.

PHILIPPIANS 2:13

THOUGHTS FOR REFLECTION

Now is a good time to ask yourself: What will help me grow closer to Christ? What seems to impede my spiritual progress? Where do I spend much of my time? Is that investment of time helping me to live a holier life? Eliminate the time you waste on trivial or even hurtful distractions and you may find the time for daily Mass, praying a daily Rosary, and spiritual reading. Instead of wasting time "decompressing" by watching hours of television and surfing the Web when you get home after a hard day at work, or after you put the kids to sleep, why not spend that time reading the Bible for a few minutes, or do as Jesus told us to do—go to your

room and in the quiet and solitude pray to your Father? Think about it. If you added just 15 minutes of prayer to your day every day, at the end of the year you would have spent nearly four days in prayer. Now four days may not sound like a lot, but ask yourself how much time you are really giving to God every year. For many of the people in the world, it's closer to four minutes than four days.

Downsize and simplify the distractions and chaos in your life, and replace that time with more prayer.

Chapter 2

Don't Look Back

Blessed is the man who endures trial, for when he has stood the test he will receive the crown of life which God has promised to those who love him.

JAMES 1:12

During my undergraduate years, while I was studying business at Arizona State University, I enrolled in a psychology course called the Rat Lab. Among other things, we learned about behavior modification by training a large black sewer rat to press a lever, which turned on a light in its cage. The rat was rewarded with a drop of water or a bit of food. During the second half of the course, all the students in the class were instructed to apply this behavior modification technique in their lives in order to help correct a flaw in their character. For my experiment I decided to train myself not to hit the snooze button, but to get out of bed as soon as my alarm sounded. Getting up im-

mediately each morning was difficult; in the cold, dark hours of the early morning it was tempting to roll over and sleep a little longer.

Looking back on that psychology class, I see how well those lessons prepared me for my spiritual walk in life. Following the retreat that changed my life, many times I resolved to spend more time reading the Bible, to go to Mass during the week, to pray the Rosary daily, and to allocate time for morning prayer. I would begin with the best intentions, but invariably within days of starting I would find some reason that I couldn't continue. I think we've all been in that situation. Somehow we fall short, and, in spite of our desire to grow closer to Christ, we allow distractions and a lack of discipline to thwart our plans. We hit the snooze button.

How can you develop a more disciplined focus on God and a more dedicated prayer life? First of all you have to die to yourself. You're probably saying, "Well, Tom, that's it, huh? That's all I have to do is die!?" Not literally; let me explain.

How often are you driven by your own wants and desires? Be honest. Come on, now. The correct answer is, nearly all the time. We have basic human needs. We need food, shelter, sleep, and, to be perfectly frank, we want to feel accepted by others, too. Whether or not acceptance is a good thing or a bad thing, we need it

nonetheless. We need to know we belong and that we matter.

But what I mean when I say you have to die to yourself is that you have to shift your priorities and your focus away from yourself and onto God and others. It means setting aside your own wishes and wants in order to serve our Lord and others as best you can. This is also called "being docile to the Holy Spirit." Isn't it difficult? Sure, at first, but many people out there do it instinctually, namely good parents. Anyone who has children knows that a part of you dies when your child is born. That old life in which you did whatever you wanted whenever you wanted to is essentially over. You shift focus. You serve. You provide. You love. You do what God does. Though it's tough to feel this way when your child is keeping you up at three a.m. with a stomachache, children are the greatest blessings because they give us insight and practice into how God, our Father, treats us.

The stories of the saints are filled with examples of selflessness. Consider Saint Elizabeth of Portugal (1271–1336). As a queen she had power, respect, luxury. Her life sounds like a fairy tale. But it wasn't. Her husband, whom she loved, was flagrantly unfaithful to her. In addition to their own children, he fathered seven illegitimate children with his various mistresses. Then

he brought them all into the palace and insisted that Elizabeth raise them. It was an outrageous demand, but out of love for her husband and affection for these poor kids—who were blameless in this family mess— she put aside her own feelings and showed herself to be a long-suffering wife and loving stepmother. Now that is an example of dying to self.

Now, looking back, I think maybe a part of my problem with my faith was that I didn't want to give up all those things I thought made me a man. My fast-paced work, my faster car, and my even faster thought process created constant traffic inside my head—worries racing about, all of them centered on me. I thought all those things made me a man, but downsizing and simplifying shifted my focus toward God and helped me to learn to shine a light on my family and others. My old self had to die, and in the process I went from being a man of the world to being a better Catholic husband, father, friend, and businessman.

The second thing you must do is take advantage of the tremendous graces available to you in the sacraments such as Communion. Saint Angela of Foligno is very eloquent on this topic: "If we but paused for a moment to consider attentively what takes place in this sacrament, I am sure that the thought of Christ's love for us would transform the coldness of our hearts into a

fire of love and gratitude." Personally, I don't think it's a coincidence that I was in the presence of the Blessed Sacrament when my reversion began. Again we need to keep in mind that I didn't have much to do with it. All I did was show up, and the Holy Spirit did the rest. There will be plenty of times when we go to Communion or confession and nothing seems to happen. Sometimes we leave Mass or afternoon confession feeling not much better off than we were before we entered the church. Yet I've learned to believe more fully in what the Nicene Creed calls "the visible and the invisible." Just because I can't always see or feel a visible change doesn't mean that an unseen transformation isn't occurring inside my soul. Think of dropping a seed into good soil. You come back the next day and nothing appears different. The day after that, nothing new. The day after that, the same. Well, you get the picture. But a couple of weeks later, you start to see a sprig of life pushing out of the ground! Aha, new life. What Dante called *la vita nuova*!

Trusting in God is easier said than done. Well, sure it is. I'm not going to lie to you. It takes effort. But so do all great things in life. That's just the way it is. But it can be done. The saints prove that it is possible to honor Our Lord and love and serve Him with "all

your heart, and with all your soul, and with all your strength."

Right about now you're probably thinking that it was easier for the saints in centuries past, when society was not so corrupt and aggressively secular, when life wasn't so complicated, when there were fewer temptations. Any student of history can tell you that the times have always been difficult. It is important to remember that you are called to be holy at this time in history, precisely in the place that God has planted you.

When you honor God by turning from sin and taking even small steps toward Him with a sincere heart, your Heavenly Father, like the father in the Parable of the Prodigal Son, comes running the rest of the way to meet you to overwhelm you with His unequaled love and mercy.

Now, just a warning. There will be times when there will be roadblocks. The devil is constantly trying to trip us up, to distract us from God, to get us to take our eyes off heaven. He knows each of our specific and most vulnerable weaknesses and will dish up customized temptations in an effort to get each one of us to fall, to drift away from God and turn back to our former lives. He doesn't want us to become holy. And the devil certainly doesn't want us to be saved, or for us to

help someone else to be saved. He is a liar, a deceiver, and incapable of love. But he wants our souls more than anything else, and he'll stoop to anything to get them.

There is no clearer example of this than the story of Lot's wife in the Old Testament. As you may recall, God was planning to rain fire down upon the town of Sodom, where the people were steeped in sin. God sent two angels to bring Lot and his family out before God destroyed the city, but Lot and his family were hesitant to leave—they loved their home. In the end the angels had to drag the family out of doomed Sodom. The angels ordered Lot, his wife, and his two daughters to run for their lives and not look back. But Lot's wife did not obey God. With a sorrowful heart for what she was giving up, Lot's wife turned to look at Sodom burning. As punishment for disobeying God and turning her attention back to her former life, Lot's wife was turned into a pillar of salt.

Lesson learned: Don't look back at the old way of doing things. Keep moving forward with your gaze fixed on God and heaven.

In chapter 17 of the Gospel of Luke, Jesus assures us that He has come to rescue us from this fallen world, and he warns us, "Remember Lot's wife" (Luke 17:32). Christ is urging us not to long for our old sins or to love this life on earth more than the prospect of an eternity

with Him in heaven. Conversion is difficult, but "all things are possible with God" (Mark 10:27). I learned these lessons in the months and years following the men's retreat that put me back on the right course, home to Jesus and His Church.

Before leaving the retreat, I had committed myself to going to Mass each morning at my neighborhood parish, St. Anne in Gilbert, Arizona. It was at daily Mass that I felt God was re-forming me, teaching me, healing me. As I started to learn, or rather relearn, my Catholic faith, I began to truly appreciate as if for the first time the Mass, the Eucharist, the Adoration of the Blessed Sacrament, the sacrament of Reconciliation, the Rosary and Chaplet of Divine Mercy, the sacrifice of Jesus for my sins, and the example and intercession of the Blessed Mother and the saints.

The Bible became the inspiring road map for my life. It had just what I needed to navigate the obstacles in my personal and my professional life. Whenever I needed them most, God's words from Scripture would come to mind. On many busy mornings, as I was on my way to Mass, I would debate skipping Mass that day and going straight to work. Then the following words would resonate in my mind: "Seek first his kingdom and his righteousness, and all these things shall be yours as well" (Matthew 6:33). So I went to Mass.

Once I trusted in Jesus, my work days went exceedingly well. All the knots were unknotted. Everything ran much more smoothly. The other two Scriptures that continued to surface in my heart were: "The harvest is plentiful, but the laborers are few" (Matthew 9:37); and "Every one to whom much is given, of him will much be required" (Luke 12:48). I knew I needed to keep moving forward with God.

At this time I was also growing to love the gentle, uncomplicated theology of Saint Thérèse of Lisieux, aka, the Little Flower. Saint Thérèse, a Doctor of the Catholic Church, was a young Carmelite nun who developed a method for growing in holiness that she called "the Little Way." She taught that even the most mundane task, if done for love of God, is pleasing to Him and helps us grow in holiness. She summed up her method with a quote that has often been attributed to her: "At every moment, do what love requires." Saint Thérèse's simple yet profound Little Way has appealed to Catholics around the globe. Since her canonization in 1925, she has been one of the most beloved saints.

By studying the saints, our brothers and sisters who have gone before us, I realized how much they could enrich my life. The saints have become my spiritual guides, and I have come to realize how desperately I need their guidance.

The time immediately after my reversion was like a honeymoon, but that did not last. The devil could not accept my profound change of heart and that now I was on God's team. Then one day the headline on the front page of the *Phoenix New Times* read: "White-collar Criminals," and the story referred to an investigation into the business practices of my biggest television client. Given their unethical business practices, I felt I could not work with this client any longer. Dropping this business would mean a major financial sacrifice for me and my family, as the fees from this client constituted one-third of my annual income.

What should I do? Here was the first major test of my newly rediscovered faith, and I did not make my decision until I was pulling into my client's parking lot: I decided to honor God by severing my business relationship with this client.

In addition to promising to attend daily Mass, I had made another promise to God: I vowed to be more generous in my gifts to charity. God had been blessing me and my family with a significant income, yet each week I was putting only a couple dollars into the collection basket. Now that I understood that all my blessings had come from the Lord, I was eager to demonstrate my gratitude by writing a check in five figures. After my television client and I went our separate

ways, doubt entered my mind, and I heard: "You can't afford to write such a large check to charity. You've lost one-third of your income. You have a wife and three young girls at home to take care of. Don't you want to be a good husband and father?" For the first time I discerned that this was not God's whisper; it was the noise of the one Jesus called "the father of lies" (John 8:44). Before any second thoughts could take hold, I drove straight to my parish and wrote the check. Leaving the parish office a little shaken, I still knew in my heart that God was guiding me in the right direction, and that if I continued to try to grow closer to God through attending Mass, receiving the sacraments, and praying frequently, I would remain on the right path.

However, there was more pruning to be done. Other business clients and even some of my colleagues tried to entice me back into my old sinful life. I could not risk the temptation and pulled back from these business associates, too. Soon my small advertising agency was left with just one client that was generating only three hundred dollars a month in income.

During the retreat I had come to understand that the clutter of our possessions can distract us from time we should be spending with God. So Tricia and I put our vacation home in Flagstaff up for sale.

One night, not long after we decided to sell the

house, we received a phone call from a friend. He and his family were staying at our mountain home. They had been out for the day, and when they returned they found that a car had crashed through the front of our house and come to a stop in our kitchen. Thank God, our friends were not in the house at the time. No one was hurt. In fact, there was no driver in the car—the high school girl who was responsible for the car was visiting friends and had forgotten to put on the parking brake, and her car had rolled down the hill into our house.

The next morning I drove up to assess the damage. The insurance adjustor was waiting for me in the driveway. So was the high school girl, along with her mother. Soon about a dozen of our neighbors came over. The girl sobbed as she asked for my forgiveness. Her mother was concerned that I intended to file a lawsuit, but I assured her that was never a consideration for me. "It's okay," I said to the girl. "It was an accident."

"Why aren't you mad at me?" the girl asked.

"Well," I said, "a couple weeks ago I would have been very upset, and would have come unglued. But I just went on a retreat with my parish where I felt God's love and mercy like never before. I'm beginning to see things differently now. You made a mistake, and

I certainly want you to know I understand, and I forgive you."

In 1 Peter 3:15 we read, "Always be prepared to make a defense to any one who calls you to account for the hope that is in you, yet do it with gentleness and reverence." That brief statement in the driveway was my first "elevator pitch" for Catholicism—a concise, personal testimony of the undeniable and remarkably tangible positive place that the Catholic faith now occupied in my life. As you begin to draw people back to the Church, you'll discover that the trials and triumphs you experience on your faith walk matter to other people, because they are experiencing the same setbacks, failures, successes, and joys. The best evangelizers are good at what they do because they make an effort to relate to their audience by sharing their common life experiences.

That unfortunate event at my vacation home taught me a valuable lesson: We must learn to praise God in all things, even our trials. Had I not accepted God's will or grace to calm my heart on that retreat, when I heard the bad news about my vacation home those dozen people might not have heard the good news about Jesus, and how faith can change lives.

That accident taught me to surrender to Divine Providence. It taught me patience and obedience. It

taught me not to look back at my old way of living. And it presented me with an opportunity to give testimony to a dozen neighbors about God's plan for our happiness. As Saint Paul reminds us in Romans 8:28, "We know that in everything God works for good with those who love him, who are called according to his purpose."

Following these events, God's amazing plan for me began to come into clearer focus. I understood I was being called upon to center my life on God, to work to help Catholics come home to the Church, and never to look over my shoulder with longing upon what might once have seemed to me to be the "glamour" of my old passions. These lures had derailed the relationship with God that I had valued when I was a child.

Normally Our Lord asks us to give a Christian witness through our ordinary lives, engaged in the same ways of earning a living, tackling the same concerns as other folk. We have to act in such a way that others will be able to say, when they meet us: This man is a Christian, because he does not hate, because he is ready to understand, because he is not a fanatic, because he is willing to make sacrifices, because he shows that he is a man of peace, because he knows how to love.

FRANCIS FERNANDEZ,
In Conversation with God

THOUGHTS FOR REFLECTION

"How are you?"

In our fast-paced world that question has become a sort of a verbal filler. We say it to colleagues, people who help us at the checkout counter, even the grump behind the window at the DMV. Most of the time people don't answer, or they'll give us a one-word answer, "Fine." You know how many times I've heard someone respond, "Fine"? If people's lives were this fine, we wouldn't be in half the messes we are in today!

So here's something to think about. The next time you greet someone, put a little spirit behind that question, even allow the Holy Spirit to articulate the words for you. Show a little enthusiasm. And when someone asks, "How are you?" answer them, "I'm blessed. How are you?" If the person you're speaking with is a Christian, your reply will remind them that we are all connected as members of God's family. If they are not deep in faith, your answer may get them thinking about God and the many blessings they have received. This response often leads to interesting conversations, and occasionally an opportunity to pray with someone who is in need of hope.

As Pope Benedict XVI said to a congregation in

Genoa in 2008, "Help each other to live and to grow in the Christian faith so as to be valiant witnesses of the Lord. Be united, but not closed. Be humble, but not fearful. Be simple, but not naive. Be thoughtful, but not complicated. Enter into dialogue with others, but be yourselves."

Chapter 3

Fast Before You Feast

Freedom consists not in doing what we like, but in having the right to do what we ought. There is no evil to be faced that Christ does not face with us. There is no enemy that Christ has not already conquered. There is no cross to bear that Christ has not already borne for us, and does not now bear with us.

POPE JOHN PAUL II

As you progress on your journey of faith, building a firm foundation on Christ and helping other Catholics to return to the Church by becoming the best Catholic you can become, you will find it necessary to fend off distractions and pull up the weeds that threaten to choke your spiritual progress. Each of us has a unique set of sins, bad habits, "rocks and thorns" that can be eliminated only with God's grace and our diligence and discipline. In the Parable of the Sower

in the Gospel of Mark (4:1–20), Jesus likens human-kind to a fertile field and the message of the Gospel to seed. Some people ignored Christ and His message entirely. Others were enthusiastic for a time, but soon their faith withered away. Some of them had faith, but it was choked by thorns, the temptations of the world. But some seeds "fell into good soil and brought forth grain, growing up and increasing and yielding thirty-fold and sixtyfold and a hundredfold" (Mark 4:8). To grow in holiness, a Christian soul needs good soil and a firm root system, and the best way to acquire both is through the Mass, the sacraments, and regular prayer.

It takes discipline to maintain a life of prayer, but while you are nurturing your soul, remember that you are also responsible for keeping your body healthy. When beginning this mission, I realized that I wasn't exercising, sleeping, or eating in a very disciplined manner, and that some changes were in order if I wanted to have the health and the strength necessary to fulfill the task God had given me. Keep your mind, body, and soul in harmony so that you can serve the Lord and fulfill your God-given roles.

We become what we surround ourselves with—the books we read, the friends we keep, the TV shows we watch, and the amount of time we devote to God and

the sacramental life. As you develop patterns of good spiritual behavior, you will find it easier to resist temptations and live a healthier life as well.

Just a quick aside while we're talking about temptations. I would guess that oftentimes we are tempted, even as faithful Catholics, to ask, "What is the very least I can do to get into purgatory?" Too often I have been guilty of settling for purgatory! Seems like we just want to make the cut, get into this waiting room of heaven, with the least effort or sacrifice. God doesn't want us to settle for a life of mediocrity, but to love Him with all our heart, mind, soul, and strength. Father Mark Beard, a late vocation priest from Baton Rouge, Louisiana, once said, "If we aim for purgatory and miss, we end up in hell. But if we aim for heaven and fall short, at least we end up in purgatory!" See how critical it is to keep our focus on the goal, fixing our eyes on more than the consolation prize. We must constantly gaze upward, seeking heaven. If we don't, we can be caught in the whirlpool of moral relativism and secularism.

When I was in prep school, one of the math teachers presented the class with two options: Would we rather have $10,000 today or a penny today that doubles in

value every day for the next thirty-one days? So one penny doubles to two, two cents doubles to four, and so on over thirty-one days. Most of my classmates took the quick cash, the instant gratification, but in doing so they settled for much less than the $10.7 million payoff from that penny that kept doubling daily for thirty-one days. This little brainteaser illustrates that too many of us are eager to grasp a small pleasure today, rather than invest the time to acquire an infinitely greater reward later.

The same is true with spreading the faith. Imagine that you become the best person of faith you can become and you reach out to one Catholic who may be wavering in his or her faith, and you help that person. Then that person reaches out to one Catholic, and then that person reaches out to another Catholic . . . well, there's no telling where this domino effect of goodwill would end, but I have a hunch that soon Sunday Mass would be a lot more crowded.

The same is true in your private life. You could spend a couple hours watching television tonight, or you could read a great Catholic book that will help you grow in faith. You could text your friends, or you could say a Rosary for someone who needs your prayers. And imagine how your life would change for the better if

rather than dreaming of how to make more money you dedicated just one hour a week to Eucharistic Adoration.

Blessed Pope John Paul II spent a good part of his pontificate reminding us to go deeper into our faith and to keep our focus on Jesus. Remember the story in Matthew 14:22–33 of Peter walking on the water toward Christ? One night Peter was fishing with some of the apostles when they saw Christ walking toward them on the water. Suddenly filled with zeal, Peter asked Jesus if he could walk across the water to meet him. "Come," Jesus said. So Peter climbed out of the boat and he began to walk on water. When he became afraid, he took his focus off Christ, got distracted, and began to sink. "Lord, save me," Peter cried. Jesus grabbed his hand, pulled him up, and together they stepped into the boat. "O you of little faith," Jesus said, "why did you doubt?"

When we take our eyes off Jesus, we always sink. God reminds us to make choices that will nourish our souls, such as frequent attendance at Mass, frequent reception of the sacraments, spending more time in prayer and reading the Bible, and being more generous in serving others who are in need. Like taking daily doses of vitamins and eating a healthy diet, all these religious practices add up, feeding our souls, helping us

to stay close to Christ, and enabling us to grow in holiness. In the tumult of each day, we can be tempted to avert our gaze from Christ and back to our short-term comforts, financial security, and our focus on doing our own will. As Proverbs 4:23 reminds us, "Keep your heart with all vigilance; for from it flow the springs of life."

I remember a time when I was lamenting over something I had left behind, and began to look back. In my materialistic days before my conversion, I really loved nice cars. One afternoon that lure from my past began to pull me back. As I was driving home from a ministry trip, a nice Lexus pulled up next to me at a traffic light. This was the IS 250 model, the little Lexus, and only a few thousand dollars more expensive than my more practical Toyota Camry. I began wondering what it would be like to drive a Lexus again, and thinking about making a visit to the dealership.

While ogling the Lexus beside me, I decided to discuss with God the potential of my getting a car like that. I began my frivolous, one-sided dialogue by reminding God how this particular model wasn't very big, was fairly economical on gas, and that it cost only a few thousand dollars more than my Camry. After all, that particular model of Lexus wasn't very showy, so owning one wouldn't be too boastful.

As I was convincing myself that my loving Father in heaven might want His son Tom to enjoy this special treat, I decided to try to stack the deck with God. I began playing "Let's Make a Deal" with Him. Here was my prayer: "Lord, if you don't want me to have this little Lexus—which is relatively inexpensive, economical on gas, and not very showy—make it abundantly clear to me—as if you were hitting me over the head with a two-by-four! Otherwise, I think I will visit the dealership this weekend. Amen."

Within a few blocks of the intersection where the Lexus had pulled up alongside me, I pulled into a shopping complex to get a haircut. After walking in I was told there would be a five-minute wait, so I began shuffling through the magazine rack to find something to read. My fingers stopped at a colorful car enthusiasts' magazine featuring a very nice-looking car on the front cover. It was the December 2009 issue of *Automobile* magazine. After somewhat coveting the extremely phenomenal-looking car on the front cover, my eyes glanced up, and I was shocked to read the caption: "Satanic Lexus."

What a headline! Now, I'm not saying messages like

this occur all the time, but I felt like God was certainly making it *abundantly clear to me—as if he were hitting me over the head with a two-by-four*—that I did not need that car! This car was not part of His plan for my life, nor would it be a benefit to me on my spiritual path at that time. It would be a distraction. (By the way, if you are driving a Lexus, this story doesn't necessarily mean you need to sell your beautiful car; this was just the message God was giving to me at that time in my life.)

However, from time to time we are called to sacrifice something we want. Often this is an invitation from God to turn away from one of the petty pleasures offered by secular society and discover the "pearl of great price," the source of lasting happiness, Jesus Christ. When we make this choice, we are heading toward the greatest good.

People in our society have increasingly become distracted with things of the world that eventually lead us farther away from God and deeper into secular pursuits. *U.S. News and World Report* ran an article on the widening divide in America between people of faith and secular humanists, some of whom are not merely indifferent to religion but openly hostile to it. The spiritual battle is getting tougher, the distractions more plentiful and frequent, yet you and I are called through

baptism to become heroes of the faith. With more faithful apostles serving Christ and helping others, our society will truly blossom.

When you reach out to the under-churched and the unchurched, you cannot know the impact you may have on their lives, their souls, their families. Parents who rarely if ever take their children to Mass may, through your efforts, bring their family back into the Church. You may have done something that will affect that family for generations. Do not be shy about sharing the mercy of Jesus with others. Never give up, because countless souls are depending on you. In 2006, while speaking to bishops from Ontario, Pope Benedict XVI pinpointed why evangelization is so vital: "The fundamental task of the evangelization of culture is the challenge to make God visible in the human face of Jesus," he said.

If you invite someone to return to the Church and your invitation is rebuffed, don't despair. Pray instead. The best thing you can do for those who are away from the Church is to listen to them, show them love, and, most of all, pray for them. At times prayer can seem so inconsequential, but it has very real effects. Big things happen when you pray. History and the lives of the

saints verify this truth again and again. Consider the example of Saint Monica. Although she had raised her son Augustine in the Church, when he went away to university he joined a pagan cult and took a mistress. Monica prayed ceaselessly for her son to return to the fullness of the Catholic faith. It seemed hopeless, but after almost twenty years of being away from the Church, the once promiscuous, proud, obstinate Augustine repented. He went on to become a priest, a bishop, and a theologian. In fact, the theological writings of Saint Augustine are among the most influential in the history of the Church, second only to the epistles of Saint Paul the Apostle. And while all the credit goes to God, you have to believe there was great power in Saint Monica's prayers.

We have to show everyone that Christ is still alive by living heroically the events of our daily lives. The apostolic vocation which we all received at Baptism means giving witness in word and deed to the life and teaching of Christ. People said of the early Christians, See how they love one another! The pagans were really edified by this behavior and those who conducted themselves in this way had favor with all the people, as the Acts of the Apostles tell us.

FRANCIS FERNANDEZ,
In Conversation with God

THOUGHTS FOR REFLECTION

God calls His disciples to choose the greatest good, the long-term benefit, to fast before we feast. Archbishop Fulton Sheen once said: "Never forget that there are only two philosophies to rule your life: the one of the cross, which starts with the fast and ends with the feast. The other of Satan, which starts with the feast and ends with the headache."

What can you fast from today that will make it possible for you to feast later in your spiritual life? What small actions can you take every day to grow in faith? I am a firm believer that where you put your focus is where you end up in life. If you're driving a car and you mistakenly focus on the wall in a long tunnel and not on the road in front of you, well, you're going to slam into that wall. In the same way, we should wake every day with the intention of putting aside something that doesn't help us grow closer to Christ and our goal of heaven. When you begin to focus on the longer-term benefits of growing in faith, guess what? You'll start doing just that. I think that one of our greatest failings isn't that we're bad people or that we do bad things, but that we forget very easily to keep focused on our ultimate goal of heaven and the discipline of doing

Chapter 4

Ask, Seek, Knock

[Jesus said,] "Follow me and I will make you fishers of men."

MARK 1:17

Are there second chances in life? The Bible affirms that there are many second chances, thanks to the mercy of God. Consider the case of Saint Peter. He was the most prominent of the apostles, the man to whom Christ gave the keys to the Kingdom of Heaven, the man Christ chose to be the first pope. Peter and his fellow apostles James and John formed Jesus's inner circle; they were Our Lord's closest friends. On the night Jesus was arrested, James fled with the other frightened apostles, and three times Peter denied that he knew Jesus—and he did so within Christ's hearing. John remained with Jesus. At the foot of the cross the next day, when Jesus was dying on Mount Calvary, John and the Blessed Mother were present, along with

more good things. It's easy to make a commitment to change your life. It's another thing to *remember* to pray for God's gift of grace so you will stick to that commitment with fortitude. So keep that in mind when you wake up every morning. By remembering, disciplining yourself to journey deeper into your faith, then you will be more effective in helping yourself and others come home to Christ.

Mary's sister, Mary the wife of Clopas, and Mary Magdalene. Peter was nowhere to be found. Nevertheless our Lord gave Peter another chance to fulfill his vocation, to live the plan that God had prepared for him.

Immediately after this triple denial, Peter was filled with remorse and ran off into the night, weeping. His contrition was sincere, and that is why, after His Resurrection, Jesus showed mercy to Peter (contrast this with Judas who betrayed Jesus as well but who never repented). In John 21:15–17 we read that three times Christ asked Peter, "Do you love me?" Each time Peter responded, "Yes, Lord; you know that I love you." Those three statements of love canceled out the three denials Peter had made in the high priest's courtyard. In response, Christ confirmed Peter in his office as head of the Church. "Feed my lambs," Jesus said. "Feed my sheep." And that is exactly what Saint Peter did. You and I are called to feed Jesus's sheep, too.

Like Saint Peter, we are called upon to share the mystery of the Divine Mercy of God with others and tell the world that we serve a God of love, who because of His forgiving heart is always eager to give unlimited second chances to anyone who is repentant and seeks His forgiveness.

One morning, while praying before Mass, I remembered a pastor had suggested that we should pray

every day that we might be an instrument to lead someone closer to Christ. So that morning I asked God to use me that day to bring someone—anyone, I wasn't picky—closer to his Son, Jesus. After Mass ended, the little Vietnamese lady seated next to me leaned over and asked if I would help her son. We went to the narthex to talk, so as not to disturb a group who had stayed after Mass to pray the Rosary.

With great anguish, this lady told me that her son had been away from the Church for nearly twenty years. She asked if I would invite him to Mass. It's always surprising how quickly the Lord answers our prayers when it's something He wants done. The mother added a special request—that I not tell her son that his mama had sent me, because it would embarrass him and perhaps make him angry with her. When I asked where I could meet her son, she said, "He works in a nail store." She meant that her son worked at a women's manicure salon. She told me her son's name was Jimmy. I went home, picked up some Catholic leaflets, then drove to the nail salon. Walking through the door, I spotted my friend's son immediately. I confess, I was a little nervous, but I said, "Somebody who loves you, God Himself, and I want to invite you back to the Catholic Church." What followed was silence, absolute silence, for what seemed to me to be an eternity. Finally Jimmy

said, "Well, it's nice of you to invite me, but I don't need church because I find God in nature. I'm a professional fisherman, and I fish nearly every day, and I feel close to God when I'm outdoors."

Not very eloquently I agreed that we certainly can find God in nature, since God created nature. But I went on to say that Jesus gave us a Church so that we could help one another get to heaven. With the world being so complex, and life so difficult, it's important for us to stick together as a Catholic family. Furthermore, it has always been Jesus's desire that we should receive Communion and the sacrament of Reconciliation frequently to help us on our journey.

When we said our good-byes, I wasn't sure if I had helped or not.

From time to time I dropped in to talk with Jimmy, and we developed a bit of a friendship. Twice I invited him to Mass, but he never showed up. Nonetheless, I tried to be optimistic. I remembered something the great Dominican preacher Saint Vincent Ferrer once said: "If you truly want to help the soul of your neighbor, you should approach God first with all your heart. Ask him simply to fill you with charity, the greatest of all virtues; with it you can accomplish what you desire." So I prayed for Jimmy with all my heart, and then I waited to see what God would do.

Finally one Sunday morning Jimmy called to say that he would join me at Mass that day. Given his track record, I was not optimistic, but this time he did show up. "Everything's changed," he told me. "I went fishing like I always do on Sunday morning, but this time I fished a crucifix out of the water. Do you think it was a sign?" I was both dumbfounded and elated. "God didn't just give you a cross," I said. "He gave you a Roman Catholic crucifix to show you which Church to come home to."

Then he asked, "Where is the box?" It took me a minute to realize Jimmy wanted to go to confession. I led him to the sacristy where the priest was vesting for Mass, and introduced Jimmy. The priest led him to a side chapel where he heard his confession before going to the altar to say Mass. That morning the prayers of a Vietnamese mother were answered—her son returned to the Church and the sacraments after being away for twenty years.

We stayed in touch. When Jimmy got married, Tricia and I were invited to the nuptial Mass. When he got back from his honeymoon, he stopped by our house to show us the wedding photos. While Tricia and our girls were looking at the pictures, Jimmy pulled me aside into the kitchen to say, "Tom, I have something to share with you that you don't know. My mom and I

are so grateful that you invited me back to church." I replied, "You're welcome; it's no big deal." Jimmy corrected me, saying, "Oh yes, it is a big deal, and you don't know the whole story. I was in the Chinese mafia in Los Angeles and got arrested for major felony crimes against society. I went to a federal penitentiary and served my sentence for the last fifteen years." Upon hearing that, I turned ashen white and felt like all the blood had rushed out of my body. I thought, "Thank goodness I didn't know about this ahead of time! I probably would have chickened out!"

Then Jimmy said, "I want to tell you, I'm so grateful, because in prison I almost committed suicide, and there were a lot of other issues. But I want you to know that in prison the inmates had time to talk about Jesus and share their faith. But now that I'm out, everybody's too busy; nobody takes the time to talk about God with other people. Thank you for taking the time to invite me back. That changed my life."

Jimmy's comments hit my heart, and I realized later that there are millions of Jimmys in the world, countless struggling souls who never grew up with much faith, or who left the Church for whatever reason. You and I need to pray for them and help these Catholics come home. We cannot be afraid to do so, as our fear of failure or fear of offending others impedes Christ's

mission for the salvation of souls. The Good Shepherd reminds us that the upside of one soul responding positively and coming home to Jesus and His Church far outweighs the downside of a few people who may reject our faith-sharing overture. Jesus promised us, "Ask, and it will be given you; seek, and you will find; knock, and it will be opened to you. For every one who asks receives, and he who seeks finds, and to him who knocks it will be opened" (Matthew 7:7). Don't be shy about asking someone if they would like to return to the faith. Don't be afraid to seek out the lost sheep. Trust that our Lord is already knocking on the door of their heart; your invitation may be the final push they need to open the door and let Christ in.

So what happened here? I prayed to help bring someone closer to Christ, and I was willing to serve. What happened? Jimmy's life was changed forever, and, thankfully, I got to witness this great adventure from God!

This is all God's work; it had little to do with me. Through this experience I learned how powerful our willingness to serve is to God. Think of the millions of struggling souls, souls who might respond to a kind word about how much God loves them. Let's go to God for the grace to be a positive influence in the lives of these souls. *Ask* God for the strength, the fortitude, and

the heroism to do the right thing. *Seek* by being present to the people around you. *Knock* on the proverbial doors of other people's hearts, by helping them to come closer to Christ.

Saint Paul in 2 Timothy 2:24–25 tells us: "And the Lord's servant must not be quarrelsome but kindly to every one, an apt teacher, forbearing, correcting his opponents with gentleness. God may perhaps grant that they will repent and come to know the truth." If you are constantly getting into arguments about someone's religious practice (or lack thereof), you are obstructing your efforts to help them come home. Of course you are convinced of the truth, goodness, and beauty of the faith, but express your conviction gently. You are called to love people into heaven, not argue them into submission.

> *My brethren, if any one among you wanders from the truth and some one brings him back, let him know that whoever brings back a sinner from the error of his way will save his soul from death and will cover a multitude of sins.*
>
> JAMES 5:19–20

THOUGHTS FOR REFLECTION

Don't try to impress others with your eloquence, or win an argument with a laundry list of facts. You may win the argument, but you may also lose a friend. People want to be heard, they want to be loved, and they will be more open if they see Christ in you. So ask God for the gifts of kindness, compassion, and gentleness. Seek a way to bring these gifts to another's door and then knock and offer these gifts in any way you can.

Chapter 5

Embrace the Mystery, Discover the Adventure

The fundamental objective of the formation of the lay faithful is an ever-clearer discovery of one's vocation and the ever-greater willingness to live it so as to fulfill one's mission. . . . The lay faithful, in fact,"are called by God so that they, led by the spirit of the Gospel, might contribute to the sanctification of the world, as from within like leaven, by fulfilling their own particular duties. Thus, especially in this way of life, resplendent in faith, hope and charity they manifest Christ to others."

POPE JOHN PAUL II

Years ago, during a motivational sales training class, the speaker drew a large iceberg on the board. Near the top he sketched a wavy line indicating the surface of the ocean. Then he pointed to the large

mass beneath the waves and asked the class, "What is this?" Someone answered, "The bottom of the iceberg." The speaker said, "Yes, but it's more accurate to say that this is the unseen potential of the iceberg. What we see is only ten percent of the iceberg, but ninety percent of its mass is a bit of a mystery, isn't it?"

We are a lot like that iceberg: Much of who we are lies below the surface. You and I are utilizing only a fraction of the potential God has implanted in us. Imagine how our lives would change, how the world would benefit, if we began to exercise the other ninety percent of our blessings, gifts, charisms, and talents that lie below the surface of our personality.

People who are away from the Church suffer from an "iceberg mentality" with regard to the Church— they see only a fraction of what the Church has to offer; they have no idea how much more beauty and wonder lie below the surface, waiting to be explored.

Not long after my life-changing retreat, Jill, a colleague I had known years ago, met me for breakfast. As we were catching up on the recent events in each of our lives, I told her about my reversion experience. After I summarized some highlights from the retreat, Jill mentioned that although she was raised Lutheran, some of her other family members had been Catho-

lic, and occasionally she had thought about becoming a Catholic, too. This led us into a deeper conversation about the Church and the faith.

A few months later Jill enrolled in the Rite of Christian Initiation of Adults (RCIA) at a Catholic parish. Even before she was received into the Church, she had become an enthusiastic novice Catholic evangelist. One evening she called to ask if I would be willing to speak with a friend of hers, Michael, who had drifted away from the Church. This was only a few months after my reversion, so the idea of speaking about the faith with a complete stranger made me a bit uncomfortable. Nonetheless, I agreed to speak with Michael. I thought I would just speak from my heart and trust that God would give me the right words to say.

The next day Michael called. The prospect of talking about such a delicate topic as faith with a stranger had made me ill at ease, but with God's help the conversation flowed naturally. After a forty-five-minute conversation, he said, "I'm coming back. I've needed to do this for years, and I'm convinced the good Lord is inviting me back." That was an exciting moment. Michael had made a life-changing decision, and I was grateful and humbled that the Holy Spirit had permitted me to be an instrument in his return to the Church.

—◦❯❮◦—

Jill called to thank me for talking to Michael. She mentioned how excited he was about coming back to the Church after having left when his children were still very young. But when Jill called again two days later, her voice sounded very somber. She began by saying, "Thanks again for helping Michael, but I've got some bad news to tell you. He died this morning." In complete shock and disbelief, I said, "The guy I just talked to on the phone two days ago?" "Yeah, he just died," Jill repeated. It was hard to comprehend that this nice guy had died so suddenly. Jill continued, "But here's why I'm calling you. Not only to tell you this news—and I am grateful that you helped Michael—but we need to help his family now. They haven't been going to Mass for years either, but they want Michael to have a Catholic funeral. It's kind of complicated. The priest said he can do the wake at the funeral home, but he can't preside at the interment due to another commitment that afternoon. He told me a layman would be allowed to say the committal prayers at the graveside, so will you do this service for the family?" I thought Jill was kidding. Nevertheless, I agreed to help in any way possible. Out of obedience to Church teachings, I wanted to double-check with my pastor regarding a layperson

leading a graveside service. So the next morning after Mass, I went into the sacristy and asked Father Doug if this was permissible. When he said it was, I started to feel clammy all over. "Well, what do I do and what prayer book do I use?" I asked. "Don't I need to sprinkle holy water to bless the coffin and grave?" After some simple coaching from Father Doug, I called Jill to confirm that I would lead the burial prayers. Again this was really pushing me beyond my comfort zone, but it seemed that Michael's family didn't have any other better options.

"Wait, there's another strange wrinkle to the story," Jill said. "Michael's son, Keith, had just been put in jail yesterday night. He was accused of murder. His sister, Heather, asked if you and I could go to the jail with her to tell Keith that his dad died." I told my wife what had happened, then climbed into my car and headed for the county jail in downtown Phoenix. The adrenaline was pumping in my veins, but I also felt nauseous and nervous.

At the jail, Jill explained the circumstances of Michael's sudden death to the clerk and introduced me as the family's spiritual advisor. Before entering the area where the inmates were held, I was required to remove my watch and my wedding ring and put them along with my wallet in a basket; I could claim my belongings

when I was ready to leave the building. At that moment I felt bare and somewhat helpless.

As we walked down the narrow, gray halls, my stomach churned. More than any other time in my life, I felt completely out of my element. We were led into a large room with several tables and picnic-style benches. Heavy iron bars covered all the windows. The guard instructed us to sit and wait at one of the tables. After the longest ten minutes of my life, we heard the clanking of bars and steel doors, and then a guard brought Keith into the room and led him to our table. His sister sat quietly on one end of the bench, Jill in the middle, with me seated on the other end. His sister sobbed, and with a shaky voice she told her brother that their dad had passed away after a massive heart attack. As she was telling him the horrific news, Keith looked at me and said, "Who the hell are you?" Instantly feeling completely out of place, I said, "I'm just a guy who talked to your dad a couple of days ago about church. And your dad was actually going to come back to the Catholic Church. Whether you're guilty or not, that's not my business, but there's a priest who serves here as a chaplain, and he is available to meet with you if you'd like. Your father told me you were raised Catholic, so please go see the priest, talk to him, and he'll keep everything you discuss completely confidential. Your dad

wanted to invite you back to church, because he just made the decision to return."

Saint Thomas Aquinas wrote, "To convert somebody go and take them by the hand and guide them." That's what I did in the county jail. I felt that I did what Michael wanted me to do. I invited his son, Keith, to come home to God and the Church.

Jill, Keith, and his sister spoke together for about fifteen minutes, then the guard escorted Keith back to his cell, and we left the county jail.

Two days later I went to Michael's wake and took a seat in the back of the room. A number of family members and friends, all strangers to me, came to pay their respects to Michael. After half an hour, a priest arrived; he read some short prayers then said a few words of consolation to the family. As the wake ended, I realized that Jill hadn't shown up, and I hoped that perhaps she would meet us at the cemetery.

At the cemetery, as I walked to the grave with Michael's family and friends, I looked around for Jill, but she was not there. Michael's casket lay beneath a broad black canopy. With the holy water in one hand and the Sacramentary in the other, I began to read the committal prayers, just as Father Doug had taught me a couple days before. Then it was time for Michael's eulogy. Although I had never met him in person, the

family had asked me to deliver the eulogy as well. I had decided to base the eulogy on Michael's decision to return to the Church. I said, "I think the message that Michael would want all of you to know is that God has a wonderful plan for each of your lives. Michael would want to encourage you to come home to the Church, just like he was planning to do." As the graveside service ended and everyone walked to their cars to drive to the reception, Heather and I were the last ones to leave. As Heather said a final good-bye to her dad, Jill finally arrived. She jumped out of her dented van, crying uncontrollably. "I missed everything! I missed Michael's funeral. I was in a wreck," she said. It seemed to me that circumstances had come full circle: Jill first helped others; now she was in need of consolation and support.

Later that weekend I reflected back on everything that had occurred since my breakfast with Jill: her entrance into the Church, my phone conversation with Michael, the visit to help Keith in jail, the graveside eulogy, and finally Jill's accident. "Life with God is certainly unpredictable," I thought.

Life is a mystery, like that iceberg I mentioned earlier in this chapter. We can never be certain what lies beneath the surface of our day-to-day experiences. So many plans don't go as expected, and life gets complicated. Yet with God we have purpose, and our faith

gives us hope. With God all things are truly possible. When we follow the promptings of the Holy Spirit, we are sometimes invited to share His love with others, sometimes many others, in the mission of helping Catholics come home.

Today and every day, Our Lord calls upon you and me to use our specific talents, in our particular occupations and neighborhoods, to serve Him by living and sharing our faith with those around us. Today so much emphasis is placed on making decisions based on our feelings, on not going beyond our comfort zone. But doing something that is necessary, even if it may be uncomfortable, not only builds character; it strengthens our faith and helps us to grow in fortitude. Pushing beyond your comfort zone is an act of trust in the Holy Spirit, and it is an opportunity to tap into some of your hidden potential.

> We make our Lord known through the example of our life, looking for occasions to speak out, not missing a single opportunity. Our task consists to a large extent in making the way to Christ cheerful and attractive. If we behave like that, many will be encouraged to follow it and to bring the joy and peace of the Lord to other men and women.
>
> FRANCIS FERNANDEZ,
> *In Conversation with God*

THOUGHTS FOR REFLECTION

When someone asks you to pray for them or for someone in need, pray right then on the spot! Not only does this help them with an immediate prayer, but it also helps you in some mysterious way to remember to pray for them later.

When you encounter people who tell you their problems and the worries in their lives, have courage to ask them, "How can I pray for you?" Oftentimes they have a big burden they are carrying, and your offer to pray for them will show them love and compassion. Oh, and don't forget to pray for them!

Chapter 6

Love Somebody to Heaven

Declare his glory among the nations,
his marvelous works among all the peoples!

1 CHRONICLES 16:24

So many people are in such great need of love.
The Jewish philosopher Philo of Alexandria (ca.
20 BC–ca. AD 40) said, "Be kind, for everyone you
meet is fighting a great battle." He knew that people
were hurting. In spite of appearances, in spite of the
face we show to the world, each one of us is wounded.
Too many of us try to soothe our wounds with the
"remedies" the world suggests: materialism, entertainment, hobbies, sex, food, drink, drugs. Instead of making us feel better, these things often distract us from
God and consequently leave us feeling unloved and
empty. No matter what challenges you and your family may be facing—unemployment, financial worries,

health problems, addictions, divorce—the only source of lasting hope, comfort, and security is Almighty God.

The early Christians were so caring and compassionate that their pagan neighbors marveled, "See how [these Christians] love one another." The loving-kindness of the first Christians attracted converts and built up the Church. It is no different today: everyone wants to be surrounded by loving, caring people.

It is through love that Jesus attracts souls to Himself. It is out of love that Jesus rescues lost sheep. Furthermore, Christ expects each baptized Christian to join in His soul-saving mission.

Before ascending into heaven, Jesus said, "Go therefore and make disciples of all nations" (Matthew 28:19). Ever since, the Catholic Church has understood that its primary mission is evangelization. But evangelization is not limited to missionaries in far-off lands. You and I have a mission to carry the message of the Gospel and the love of God to our family and friends, neighbors and coworkers.

Perhaps you're thinking, "My faith is private. I don't want to proselytize." Perhaps you are afraid that you don't know the faith well enough to explain it to others. But you do not have to be a theologian. What you are doing is planting the seed, and you do that not by tackling difficult doctrinal questions but by tell-

ing your own story of the good things God has done
in your life. You can talk about the prayers that God
has answered, the peace that was restored in your family, and all the other blessings that God has given to
you. If you speak from the heart, if you speak sincerely
and with love, wonderful things can happen. Don't be
afraid. Be open and pray every day that God will grant
you the grace to help lead someone to Christ, to help
love somebody to heaven. So many lay apostles are already answering this call, as are many parishes, countless priests and deacons, religious sisters, and bishops
who courageously and lovingly work together as a family to bring our brothers and sisters home. In 2006,
on the fortieth anniversary of the publication of the
Vatican II document *Ad Gentes*, Pope Benedict XVI reminded the Church that evangelization "is not something optional, but the very vocation of the People of
God, a duty that corresponds to it by the command of
the Lord Jesus Christ himself."

Before you begin speaking of the faith, listen to the
person you're about to address. What struggles or
challenges are they facing? Has your friend just gone
through a significant loss? Your effort with them will
be in vain if you spend an hour telling your friend

about the intricacies of Marian doctrine, when what they really need to hear is the Church's restorative teaching on redemptive suffering. All too often we resort to intellectual defenses for the Catholic faith when someone is struggling with a deep emotional setback that needs to be addressed altogether differently but nonetheless with the truth of the Church. Remember, nobody cares how much you know until they know how much you care. This is worth repeating: Nobody cares how much you know until they know how much you care. Don't just talk in a God-loving way. Be and exist in a God-loving way. And keep the words to a minimum.

We are all called, each in our way, to guide souls. We have to be open to the Holy Spirit and seize God's gift of opportunity. In the words of Saint Paul in 1 Corinthians 9:16, "Woe to me if I do not preach the gospel!" When the Holy Spirit gives you the opportunity to talk to someone about the faith, don't turn away. And when you give your testimony, do so with humility and compassion, not with judgment and condemnation.

Mercy is the theme of our Catholics Come Home television commercial entitled "Movie." In the opening scenes we see the deadly sins of anger, prejudice, gossip, and substance abuse. At the transitional point

right in the middle of the commercial we hear, "But Jesus didn't come to condemn the world; He came to save it." Have you ever heard better news? Remember, no matter what you have done, it's never too late to accept God's love, mercy, and forgiveness. We serve a God who offers us unlimited do-overs through the divine mercy of Jesus. Jesus's mercy is a free gift placed in front of each of us. All we have to do is accept it.

Every day, all day long, God is saying to you, "I'm here. I love you. Return to me." Most people who do not hear God's invitation are not actively rejecting Him; they are so absorbed in the distractions of the world that they are barely aware that God exists. Nonetheless, the gift of His mercy is always available, waiting for the day when those lost sheep realize how much they need it.

If members of your family are among those lost sheep who have drifted away from the Church, never stop praying for them. One of the most efficacious moments to pray for their return comes at Mass when the priest raises the chalice of the Precious Blood of Jesus during the Consecration. Remember that out of love and compassion for sinful humankind, Christ poured out His blood for the salvation of the world. He does not want to lose a single soul. So at the elevation of

the chalice, mention the names of your loved ones, put them into the Precious Blood of Jesus, and ask the Lord to bring them home.

Perhaps the greatest spiritual challenge our families face today is the battle against secular humanism. Secular humanism is defined as "humanistic philosophy viewed as a nontheistic religion antagonistic to traditional religion." Another source says that it is "a religious worldview based on atheism, naturalism, evolution, and ethical relativism," and that secular humanists are atheists who adopt "ethical relativism"—the idea that there is no absolute moral code, so we're free to adjust our ethical standards to suit each situation.

This sinister philosophy makes almost no demands. It promotes ideas that on the surface, at least, appear attractive. The cultural elites such as those in the media, some areas of academia, and many in Hollywood all tell us that this philosophy is what the intelligent, trendy people believe. It is seductive, this idea that there are no absolutes of right and wrong, that morality is one big gray area, so everyone should live in a manner that is most comfortable for them.

Even religious believers can find secular humanism hard to resist, as I knew all too well. But you must resist it. This is not the Gospel; this is not God's plan for humankind. If you find yourself too caught up in

the busyness of your daily routine, if you find yourself missing Mass and skipping your prayers, then slam on the brakes and look around, not just outwardly but also inwardly. Is there a void? I'm sure there is, and if so, then Mass, frequent reception of the sacraments, and private prayer—these are the keys to abiding in God's peace and recognizing your true purpose in this world. While it's important to love others to heaven, it's equally important to love ourselves to heaven as well, and we do this by resting in the presence of the Lord.

Do you recall the story of Jesus's visit to the home of the two sisters, Mary and Martha (Luke 10:38–42)? While Martha bustled about seeing to the meal and the table so that everything would be perfect for her guest, Mary sat at the feet of Jesus, listening to every word he said, nurturing her spiritual life. At the end of this episode Jesus reminds us, "Mary has chosen the good portion, which shall not be taken away from her" (Luke 10:42). As Christians, we need to have a finely tuned mix of both the contemplative and the active life. First, we need to be filled with God's word in Scripture, grace from the sacraments, as well as the peace and wisdom that come from contemplative prayer. Only then will we be more fully equipped to faithfully and productively carry out our active apostolic mission, guided by the Holy Spirit. We must be

filled up by means of contemplative prayer, then be active when we need to be active.

In his book, *The Soul of the Apostolate*, Dom Chautard, a French Cistercian abbot, refers to this scene in the house of Mary and Martha when he writes about people who love action for action's sake:

> *Any pretext will serve if we can only escape this discipline of our faculties: business, family problems, health, good reputation, patriotism, the honor of one's congregation, and the pretend glory of God, all vie with one another in preventing us from living within ourselves. This sort of frenzy for exterior life finally succeeds in gaining over us an attraction that we can no longer resist. Is there any reason to be surprised, then, that the interior life is neglected?*

Dom Chautard says that we can overlook the value of "living with Christ, in Christ and through Christ, and of forgetting that everything, in the plan of Redemption, is based on the Eucharistic life as much as it is upon the rock of Peter." He urges us, even during the busiest days, to slip away for a few minutes and "go and purify and rekindle [your] energy before the Taber-

nacle . . . to obtain from its Divine Guest better results for [your] work."

Accept the gift of God's mercy. Let yourself be filled with the graces of the Holy Spirit so that the light of Christ and the love of Our Heavenly Father can overflow through you to those you meet. The time is now!

As each has received a gift, employ it for one another, as good stewards of God's varied grace.

1 PETER 4:10

THOUGHTS FOR REFLECTION

When speaking with someone who is struggling with the Church's discipline or moral teachings, try a personalized version of the "feel, felt, found" technique. Here's how it goes: "With regard to Jesus's teachings on [the sanctity of life, contraception, traditional marriage, going to a priest for confession], I know how you *feel*. In fact, I [many people I know] *felt* the same way at one time. But after studying the *Catechism of the Catholic Church*, I *found* that Jesus's teaching on that subject makes perfect sense. Here's why. . . ."

This *feel, felt, found* technique allows you to be empathetic without being confrontational about the person's point of view. It is a gentle way to share the truth and guide the conversation to a more positive outcome. In doing this you take another step toward loving someone to heaven.

Chapter 7

Home for Good

So, being affectionately desirous of you, we were ready to share with you not only the gospel of God but also our own selves, because you had become very dear to us.

1 Thessalonians 2:8

When my family and I lived in Phoenix, we heard the legend of an old desert prospector who spent years chipping away inside a mountain cave, certain that at any moment he would strike gold. After years of digging he finally gave up and abandoned his claim. Then another old prospector came along, bought the claim, and started digging. He had dug only one foot into the rock when he discovered the largest gold deposit in Arizona history. By the example of these prospectors, we learn that we must never give up.

Saint Paul teaches us to persevere, to keep our eyes on Christ and never lose hope, no matter how difficult or discouraging our journey may become. And he

urges us always to be ready to carry the good news announced by Jesus Christ to our neighbors, "in season and out of season" (2 Timothy 4:2).

Not long ago I took an early morning flight from Wichita to Atlanta. Getting up while it was still dark was hard, but I consoled myself with the thought that at least I'd be comfortable on the plane; I had gotten an upgrade to first class, thanks to being a frequent flier. Unfortunately, after boarding the plane I found that we had been assigned an old aircraft that did not have a first-class section. Some of the first-class passengers lost their temper and took out their frustrations on the flight crew.

It wasn't the flight attendants' fault, and they were doing their best to make everyone comfortable. When an attendant brought me a cup of coffee, I said to her, "You know, even though we don't have a first-class section today, you're still giving all of us first-class service. Thank you so much." This flight attendant wore a name badge that read "Jessie." She smiled and said, "Thank you so much for saying that. It's been a tough morning and a rough week in general." We talked a little bit more, and then she moved on to serve the other passengers.

We were about halfway through our flight when I

saw Jessie talking with another flight attendant. They were whispering, so I could not hear what they were saying, but from her tone of voice it was obvious that Jessie was distraught. I prayed and wondered what I could do to help her. After that prayer, I felt led to take out a Catholics Come Home evangelization card from my wallet and to write on the back of it: "Jessie, the hope that you seek comes only from Jesus and His Church. God loves you! Tom."

At the end of the flight, as the crew prepared for landing, Jessie came down the aisle one last time. As she was passing my seat, she stopped and said, "I can't thank you enough for being so nice. I just really feel that we were supposed to meet. Thank you so much." Handing her the card with the message, I said, "Please read this when you get off the plane."

About a week later a letter arrived from Jessie. She wrote,

> My name is Jessie. You were on my flight, and you handed me a card with a note on the back. How did you know I was so desperately in need of that message? I want to thank you. I have not stopped crying since I read your note and went to your website. I was raised Catholic, but had been away from the Church and God for many years. I'm recently

divorced and struggling with the emptiness of being alone.
I have been searching for a man to be in my life and I have
found that man. It's God.

Jessie had gone back to Mass and came home to God that past weekend. We sent Jessie a note of encouragement and urged her to keep on this new path of faith.

A few weeks after her first letter, Jessie wrote again, saying,

I've been feeling better lately. Praying a lot and vowing to
be a good Christian. I'm making an effort to be a positive
affect on at least one person every day. Yesterday I finished
my last flight of the day after working 12 hours. My fel-
low crew members went home, while I stayed and helped a
pregnant lady with three toddlers, a cat, a stroller, and six
carry-on bags get to their next gate on time. It got me home
about an hour late, but it felt good to help somebody in need.

See how love creates a ripple effect? When we share God's love with someone, often they will pass it on, changing our world for the better. It is God's plan for us to share the love of Christ every chance we get.

Ask yourself, "Am I letting Jesus fill me with His grace so that His grace can overflow into others through me?" If not, do all that you can to align yourself with

His holy will. The way to begin is with the sacrament of Reconciliation, then add more prayer, Eucharistic Adoration, reading the Bible and holy Catholic books, and spiritual direction. God our Father has given each of us particular talents and abilities. Each of us has a specific purpose in life. Every soul is called to a unique mission that only it can fulfill. This is our Father's amazing plan for each one of His children, intricately designed so that all of us who cooperate with His will can be happy in this life and supremely happy with Him forever in heaven.

Jesus is asking you now to tell others about our Father's love. Are you ready to join the New Evangelization? Are you willing to serve in the irreplaceable role that only you can fulfill? Are you prepared to help invite nearly one billion souls into the largest family reunion in salvation history?

There's a popular Christian song on the radio by Martina McBride called "Do It Anyway" in which we are reminded that even when we don't feel like we have the time, energy, or talent, we should always do what's right and what God would want us to do at that moment. She urges us to step beyond convenience, comfort, and fear of embarrassment to "do it anyway," because serving God and others is how Christianity calls us to live every moment.

If you are still reluctant, don't be afraid. After all, you are a child of God and a friend of Jesus. As Saint Teresa of Avila once said, "All my longing was and still is that since [God] has so many enemies and so few friends that these few friends be good ones."

Francis Fernandez, in his series of books, *In Conversation with God*, encourages us to plunge deeper into our faith and be more committed in our service to others. "We have to show everyone that Christ is still alive," Fernandez writes, "by living heroically the events of our daily lives." Gandhi put it more bluntly when he said: "Oh, I don't reject Christ. I love Christ. It's just that so many of you Christians are so unlike Christ. If Christians would really live according to the teachings of Christ, as found in the Bible, all of India would be Christian today."

Let us bring Christ's compassion to the wounded souls around us. Let us take the Blessed Mother as our role model, imitating her by trying to serve the Lord with our entire heart and will. Let's look to her as the perfect example of evangelization, humility, and obedience. Mary is the living monstrance who holds up Jesus for all the world to see.

We must do the same by bringing the light of the Eucharistic Christ to a hurting world in need of great hope. God is calling you to help Catholics come home. How will you answer Him? If you and I don't share the faith, Catholicism could become *the greatest story never told.*

A new dawn is shining on our world today. A fresh springtime of hope awaits us! God is calling little souls like you and me to take part in big adventures. So join now in this mission of the New Evangelization!

Come and see what God has done:
he is awesome in his deeds among men.

PSALM 66:5

THOUGHTS FOR REFLECTION

When someone questions your desire to help souls home to the Catholic Church and asks, "What are they coming home to?" answer as follows: "They are coming home to the Church founded over two thousand years ago by Jesus Himself. Through His Church, Jesus feeds us with His own Body and Blood in the

Eucharist and forgives us through the sacrament of confession. And in spite of all our human frailties and failings, Jesus has promised us that the Holy Spirit will guide His Church and that it will endure until the end of time. There is no alternative, no second best."

Afterword

WHAT WE'VE SEEN AND HEARD

Over the years at Catholics Come Home we've heard from some of the hundreds of thousands of people who have returned to the Catholic Church, or converted to the faith. One young man left the Church and became a Muslim in his twenties, but he returned to his Catholic faith after seeing the Catholics Come Home evangomercial on television in Boston. We also learned about a young Polish immigrant in Chicago who had drifted into agnosticism during his teenage years, until he saw a Catholics Come Home ad on Polsat, the Polish language television station. He came home, too. A middle-aged Irish woman named Maggie wrote to us telling about how she came back to the Church after being away for decades, saying: "I moved to Northern Arizona from Dublin, Ireland, thirty years ago and I gave up my faith. And for a while I wasn't going to church anymore. Soon I became an agnostic. I didn't

even know if there was a God, or cared. But then I saw the commercial for Catholics Come Home and I began to weep. I went online to your website [www .CatholicsComeHome.org] and looked up my parish Mass times. And I came home after all these years." I e-mailed Maggie and started asking her a few questions, having been intrigued by her story. Maggie told me that her mother back in Dublin had never stopped praying for her return to the faith—just as Saint Monica had prayed for her son Augustine. Through God's grace and her mother's prayers, the Holy Spirit orchestrated the Catholics Come Home television ad to air at the right time to touch Maggie's heart and lead her home.

Scott, a man in his early thirties, wrote us from Colorado: "I was born Catholic, but I drifted and became an atheist. For years I called myself an atheist and said religion was irrelevant. I came across the [www .CatholicsComeHome.org] website, looked at the ads and thought that it kind of makes some sense. And I started investigating it some more." That Easter, Scott returned to the Catholic Church. Recently, we learned that Scott is now evangelizing his brother, who professes to be an atheist. Now, Scott is helping to invite his brother home, too. When one soul helps another soul, countless souls can be helped.

Next there is Henry, a college student at an interdenominational university in Tulsa. Henry was a faithful Protestant, but felt that there was something missing in his spiritual life. Henry admitted that over the last few years he had started investigating other faiths. He said, "I stumbled upon Catholics Come Home and our Spanish website [www.CatolicosRegresen.org] and started looking into Catholic teachings." Today not only is Henry a practicing Catholic, but he also completed a master's program in theology at a Catholic university and is now teaching the faith.

When we hear these stories, we see how God's grace blesses humanity. These are "God-incidences," where God is directly touching the lives of people, then using them to bring others to the fullness of faith. God wants you and me to do the same.

After airing Catholics Come Home evangelization campaigns in over thirty-five archdioceses and dioceses, we've received very encouraging and interesting reports from our diocesan partners. Most noted sizable increases in Mass attendance and participation in the sacrament of Reconciliation. Many dioceses reported a rise in volunteerism and tithing, because current Catholics felt a renewed sense of pride in their Church and stronger Catholic identity. Countless parishes cited an increase in Rite of Christian Initiation

of Adults (RCIA) inquiries from people who had seen the evangomercials. A number of parish priests and diocesan officials claim that most of the returnees they have spoken with didn't have serious reasons for leaving the Church, that most inactive Catholics don't hate the Church, and that most have not fallen completely away from God either. Many admitted that they just drifted away because life got too busy, or they had to take their kids to sporting events on Sunday. About 10 percent of the returnees said that they were divorced and didn't know whether they could still be members of the Church—wondering if they were excommunicated.

CULTURAL TRENDS AND THE MEDIA

Many think that people started to lose their focus on God and began to become self-centered beginning in the 1960s, when we entered the age of egotism, self-love, free love, experimentation with drugs, addiction to sensory entertainment, and rebellion against authority.

Looking back a decade earlier to the 1950s, we see that one of the stars of American television was Bishop Fulton J. Sheen. Some would consider him to be the godfather of the New Evangelization. Bishop Sheen's

keen wit, sharp mind, flair for the dramatic, and down-to-earth discussions of the faith won him millions of loyal viewers. His program, *Life Is Worth Living*, was the number one show in America, with higher ratings than the variety show of legendary comedian Milton Berle. Incredibly, a high percentage of non-Catholics regularly tuned in every week to watch Bishop Sheen. Can you imagine that happening today? It's hard to comprehend that a deeply religious program, let alone one starring a Catholic bishop, would lead the ratings. I doubt that secular media executives today would allow Bishop Sheen on network TV.

More than sixty years ago Bishop Sheen encouraged us to go deeper into our faith. "Really, most of us live below the level of our energy," he said. "And, in order to be happy, we need to do more. Now, we can do more spiritually and in every other way. So you see how important it is to have the mind to do all that you can do? To work to the limit of your ability. Our world is really suffering from indifference. Indifference is apathy, not caring."

Bishop Sheen challenges us to live our faith to the fullest, to aim for heaven, and to make a positive difference in the lives of others. Why? Because Jesus shows us the way, modeling mercy and compassion, even though as sinners we don't deserve His love. Christ calls us to

take up our cross daily, to put aside our selfish ways, and to follow Him. We must fight the indifference and apathy, overcome the noise and distractions that battle for our attention, our time, and our heart. If we truly love Jesus, we will honor our Lord as He pleads with us to "feed my sheep."

A couple years ago Father Henry Atem, originally from Cameroon, Africa, invited me to speak at the African Conference of Catholic Clergy and Religious in the United States (ACCCRUS), held in Atlanta. It was an awesome experience, and the priests and religious sisters from Africa who are serving in America were so filled with joy and incredibly kind to me. During the question and answer session following my speech, one of the nuns stood up and said, "Americans came to evangelize us years ago; now we are coming back from Africa to help re-evangelize America today." I thank God for these faithful witnesses who have traveled so far from home, so far from family and the comfortable familiarity of their own homelands, and made the sacrifice to help lead souls back to Christ and His Church. Our Catholics Come Home outreach of www .EncouragePriests.org is a resource that the lay faithful can use to pray for and support our priests and encourage religious vocations.

What's in it for me? and *What is the very least I can do?* A 2010 Gallup Poll found a growing divide between Church teachings and what people are *actually* doing. Gallup reported on the following key moral issues:

- *Having a baby outside of marriage:* 54 percent found it morally acceptable; only 42 percent said it was immoral.
- *Same sex relations:* 52 percent said it was morally acceptable; only 43 percent said it was immoral.
- *The death penalty:* 65 percent said it was morally acceptable; only 26 percent said it was immoral.
- *Assisted suicide:* 49 percent said it was morally acceptable; only 44 percent said it was immoral.

The old saying of "love the sinner, hate the sin" still applies here. Who would want to come back to the Church if they thought that it condemns people? When sharing Jesus's teachings, we must always speak the truth with love in order to bring more souls to Christ.

Every decade, more souls are being desensitized, negatively catechized by moral relativism and secular humanism. With each passing year, more souls veer farther from the straight and narrow path that leads

to eternal life. Eventually, additional souls will abandon the moral compass that at one time pointed them in the direction of Truth. At the farthest end of this spectrum from belief in God is atheism, and it is also on the rise in our culture. My dear friend and Catholic author Patrick Madrid, along with Kenneth Hensley, his coauthor, discusses the fallacies of atheism in his timely book *The Godless Delusion*. In large metropolitan areas like Toronto, Seattle, and Chicago, the atheists sponsor billboards and bus ads spreading Godless propaganda to our youth and the culture at large. A few examples of their messages include "There is probably no God . . . so stop worrying and start living!" Another encourages: "Go ahead, sleep in on Sunday."

As a former advertising agency executive, I'm perplexed by this. I fail to understand the atheists' economic model. In other words, if atheists don't believe in God, why would they spend their hard-earned money to convince other people *not* to believe in Him? You would think they would say, *You do your thing, and I'll do mine.* But this isn't what they're doing. I fervently believe Saint Paul was right when he wrote in his Epistle to the Ephesians 6:12: "For we are not contending against flesh and blood, but against the principalities, against the powers, against the world rulers of this

present darkness, against the spiritual hosts of wickedness in the heavenly places." In the spiritual war, we must choose sides, either serving God and putting our complete hope and trust in the saving grace of Jesus or choosing the dark way of the world. The atheists' advertising campaign shows their hand; it reveals their true motive—they are trying to lure souls away from God. The sinister forces of evil are at work in those billboards.

At this time in salvation history, Jesus is calling each one of us to pick sides and choose our path. We are called no longer to live in secular mediocrity, for we must submit to God's perfect will and aim for heaven. As faithful Catholics, we cannot live any longer in the mushy middle, in that lukewarm gray area. The time has come for us to live and serve heroically and reject the shades of gray. Our world is spiraling out of control and too many people are becoming untethered from God. Now, more than ever, is our time to join the chorus of the saints in saying, "As for me and my house, we will serve the Lord" (Joshua 24:15). Now is our time to answer Jesus's call to help rescue drifting souls, to help *Catholics come home*!

When you think of the poor who die of hunger, of victims of catastrophes and of murderous wars, your heart breaks and your pocketbook opens. And still more, your heart must break when you think that souls are dying by the millions of spiritual hunger. Jesus thirsts for these souls but they cannot go to Him, because they do not know Him.

JEAN C. J. D'ELBÉE, *I Believe in Love*

Appendix

Two thousand years ago, Saint Paul advised the Christians in Ephesus, "Put on the whole armor of God, that you may be able to stand against the wiles of the devil" (Ephesians 6:10). If Saint Paul were writing today, he might replace the term "armor" with "tool kit." That is what is assembled for you here—your complete Catholic Evangelization Tool Kit. I've listed my favorite books, which I hope will increase your faith in God and your devotion to the Blessed Mother and the saints. I've assembled a handful of my favorite Catholic quotations, which inspire me in my work of evangelization. I've collected my favorite prayers, both traditional and contemporary, that soothe my heart and mind, and feed my soul. I know that these prayers will help you to stay connected to the Holy Trinity and all the saints in heaven. I've also included a short listing of some of my favorite Catholic groups that have

blessed my life. And finally, as you prepare to bring Catholics home, I will close my book the way Bishop Fulton Sheen, the greatest American evangelist of all time, always wrapped up his television program: "God love you!"

SUGGESTED READING FOR ASPIRING CATHOLIC EVANGELISTS

Trustful Surrender to Divine Providence: The Secret of Peace and Happiness, by Jean Baptiste Saint-Jure, SJ (Charlotte, N.C.: Tan Books, 1983).

This has to be in my top-ten favorite, life-changing books of all time. Trusting God helps reduce stress, eases the workload, and brings you in close relationship with your Father in heaven. Amazingly, I even learned that God allows all things that will occur; after all, He is God and could stop certain things from happening, but God brings good even out of the bad, for our sanctification and His glory.

Deep Conversion/Deep Prayer, by Thomas Dubay (San Francisco, Calif.: Ignatius Press, 2006).

Fr. Dubay led millions of mediocre Christians from lukewarm faith to holiness. This is a favorite book of mine.

The Soul of the Apostolate, by Dom Jean-Baptiste Chautard,
OCSO (Charlotte, N.C.: Tan Books, 1977).

This is a must-read book for anyone with a vocation or
anyone who leads an apostolate (which means this book is
pretty much for everyone!). Chautard is a wise mentor, and
his writings are classic, feeding us with nutrient-rich spiritual wisdom to help in everyday situations.

I Believe in Love: Retreat Conferences on the Interior Life, by
Père Jean du Coeur de Jésus D'Elbée, trans. Marilyn
Teichert (Still River, Mass.: Saint Bede's Publications,
1983).

A small book that brings the reader on a spiritual retreat
led by the teachings of the Little Flower, Saint Thérèse of
Lisieux. Jesus thirsts for souls, and D'Elbée shows us how to
help bring more thirsting souls home to Jesus.

*Reasons to Believe: How to Understand, Explain, and Defend the
Catholic Faith,* by Scott Hahn (New York: Doubleday,
2007).

This book is a great resource for learning the whys and hows
of your Catholic faith. It is a powerful book to get into the
hands of your fallen-away Catholic or non-Catholic friends
and relatives, too. With all of these reasons to believe, it's
hard not to be convinced by the truth of the Catholic faith
by the end of this book.

*"I'm Not Being Fed!": Discovering the Food That Satisfies the
     Soul,* by Jeff Cavins (West Chester, Pa.: Ascension
     Press, 2005).

Jeff Cavins has a gift for taking complex theological concepts and explaining them so that everyone understands. As a baptized Catholic who turned Protestant pastor, then reverted back to the Catholic faith, Jeff is ideally suited to discuss why people leave the faith as well as ways to invite souls home to the Catholic Church.

*Crossing the Tiber: Evangelical Protestants Discover the
     Historical Church,* by Stephen Ray (San Francisco,
     Calif.: Ignatius Press, 1997).

Steve Ray blesses audiences across the world with his knowledge of Scripture, history, and the Catholic faith. As a convert, Steve brings a wealth of information that will help you share the faith with neighbors.

Rome Sweet Home: Our Journey to Catholicism, by Scott and
     Kimberly Hahn (San Francisco, Calif.: Ignatius Press,
     1993).

This is one of the best books ever written about a journey into the Catholic Church, from perhaps the most famous converts to Catholicism. Dr. Scott Hahn and his wife, Kimberly, lecture across the world, inspiring Catholics to go deeper into their faith.

Set Your Heart Free (30 Days with a Great Spiritual Teacher), by Saint Francis de Sales, ed. John Kirvan (Notre Dame, Ind.: Ave Maria Press, 2008).

Small, daily readings that soothe our stress, calm our anxieties, and build our trust in God. Saint Francis de Sales was a masterful evangelist, and his insights and prayers will bathe your soul with refreshment and peace.

Diary: Divine Mercy in My Soul, by Saint Maria Faustina Kowalska (Stockbridge, Mass.: Marian Press, 2002).

Who doesn't love Saint Faustina, for she brings us the Divine Mercy of Jesus Christ? One of the great Polish saints in the likeness of Saint Maximilian Kolbe and Blessed John Paul II, Faustina speaks with clarity and simplicity.

Two titles by Patrick Madrid: *Surprised by Truth: 11 Converts Give the Biblical and Historical Reasons for Becoming Catholic* (Irving, Tex.: Basilica Press, 1994); and *Surprised by Truth 2: 15 Men and Women Give the Biblical and Historical Reasons for Becoming Catholic* (Manchester, N.H.: Sophia Institute Press, 2000).

The *Surprised by Truth* series contains moving stories of people who discovered the truth of the Catholic Church and couldn't help but come home. The books answer common objections to the Catholic faith and depict in a powerfully personal way the struggles people face on their journey

home. These books make great gifts for friends and relatives who are away from the Church.

How to Win the Culture War: A Christian Battle Plan for a Society in Crisis, by Peter Kreeft (Downers Grove, Ill.: InterVarsity Press, 2002).

This book is a masterpiece for today's times, outlining a Christian battle plan for our culture in crisis. If we understand the battle going on in our society—the culture of life versus the culture of death—we are better equipped to join the effort to spread love and truth and win souls back to Christ and His Catholic Church.

Rediscover Catholicism: A Spiritual Guide to Living with Passion and Purpose, by Matthew Kelly (Cincinnati: Beacon Publishing, 2002).

Matthew Kelly is one of the most popular Catholic speakers and authors in the world. *Rediscover Catholicism* is a highly recommended book for the New Evangelization!

Wisdom from the Pulpit: A Collection of 80 Short Walks in Every Day Life, by George McKenna (Oak Lawn, Ill.: CMJ Marian Publishers, 2007).

God bless Father McKenna! Tricia and I met him and discovered this book after Mass at the Midway Airport chapel near Chicago. He served there for years. This is a wonderful

collection of inspiring homilies, more profound than most you have ever heard.

Search and Rescue: How to Bring Your Family and Friends into—or Back into—the Catholic Church, by Patrick Madrid (Manchester, N.H.: Sophia Institute Press, 2001).

The title says it all—this book is an excellent go-to resource when it comes to evangelizing the people closest to you and inviting them home to the Catholic Church. Pat Madrid gives concrete, easy-to-follow strategies for starting those often-difficult conversations with loved ones and being God's instrument to call them back to the practice of their Catholic faith.

Patience: Thoughts on the Patient Endurance of Sorrows and Sufferings, by F. X. Lasance (Elmhurst Township, Pa.: Fraternity Publishing, 1937).

A book so tiny, it will fit in the palm of one hand! A great little companion for your pocket or backpack; for reading everywhere from short flights to waiting in the carpool lane. In our busy world, we all need more patience!

Mere Christianity, by C. S. Lewis (New York: HarperCollins, 2001).

On of the most timeless and foundational books in any Christian's library. Every high-school-age student should

study the writings of C. S. Lewis, who is also author of the well-known *Chronicles of Narnia*.

Psalms: A School of Prayer, by Mark Link, SJ (Chicago: Thomas More Press, 1996).

The Psalms bring us into the heart of joy, and more deeply into contemplative prayer. God loves us, and the Psalms are love poems from our Creator. Father Link weaves them together into a wonderful collection of prayers.

Good News, Bad News: Evangelization, Conversion and the Crisis of Faith, by Father C. John McCloskey III and Russell Shaw (San Francisco, Calif.: Ignatius Press, 2007).

Evangelizing is the responsibility of *every* Catholic. Father McCloskey and Russell Shaw, some of the greatest American evangelizers today, explain how to evangelize with passion and respect for others, so you can help God change lives in the midst of our secular culture—one soul at a time.

John Paul II and the New Evangelization: How You Can Bring the Good News to Others, edited by Ralph Martin and Peter Williamson (Cincinnati: Servant Books, 2006).

This book is filled with answers to your questions about how to participate in the New Evangelization, how to evangelize young people, how your parish can get involved in evange-

lization, and much more. It is a practical and instructional guide to living out Blessed Pope John Paul II's call for the New Evangelization.

The Little Way of St. Thérèse of Lisieux: Into the Arms of Love, by John Nelson (Liguori, Mo.: Liguori Publications, 1998).

Saint Thérèse, the Little Flower, is one of my favorites! She is a Doctor of the Church whose prime charism is simplifying the most direct route to union with God. Her teachings are easy to understand and apply. Saint Thérèse is like no other saint, and she will likely become one of your favorite saints, too.

Father Elijah: An Apocalypse, by Michael O'Brien (San Francisco, Calif.: Ignatius Press, 1996).

This may be the only fictional novel on my list. Michael O'Brien is a gifted Catholic storyteller. His incredible writing style motivated me to read this 600-some-odd-page masterpiece in a mere four days! *Father Elijah* is a page-turner, filled with the realism of spiritual warfare in our day and age. Everyone to whom I've give this recommendation loves this book.

The Emerging Laity: Vocation, Mission, and Spirituality, by Aurelie Hagstrom (Mahwah, N.J.: Paulist Press, 2010).

Dr. Hagstrom is a professor of theology at Providence College who lectures on the laity as well as the gift of *welcoming* souls home to the Church.

The Interior Castle, by Saint Teresa of Avila, in *The Collected Works of St. Teresa of Avila,* vol. 2, trans. Kieran Kavanaugh and Otilio Rodriguez (Washington, D.C.: ICS Publications, 1980).

The foundress of the Discalced Carmelites and Doctor of the Church, Saint Teresa of Avila brings us deeper into the spiritual life and closer to the heart of Christ. Teresa's works, like those of her compatriot Saint John of the Cross, are filled with richness and depth. This book can help strengthen your inner life.

Whispers from the Cross: Reclaiming the Church Through Personal Holiness, by Anne, a Lay Apostle (Oak Lawn, Ill.: CMJ Marian Publishers, 2011).

Whispers from the Cross seems to touch my soul. After I read a book like this I say, "I felt like God was personally speaking to me!"

The Better Part: A Christ-Centered Resource for Personal Prayer, by John Bartunek (Modesto, Calif.: Catholic Spiritual Direction, 2011).

Mary has chosen the better part, as Scripture teaches. Father Bartunek shares incredible wisdom and spiritual direc-

tion with his readers, relating to contemplative prayer, and spiritual growth. This is deep reading, filled with pearls.

The Art of Dying Well (or How to Be a Saint Now and Forever), by Saint Robert Bellarmine (Manchester, N.H.: Sophia Institute Press, 2005).

Our goal is to be a saint, and we have a manual, a road map of sorts by an expert, a saint himself, to guide us to holiness.

The Temperament God Gave You: The Classic Key to Knowing Yourself, Getting Along with Others, and Growing Closer to the Lord, by Art and Laraine Bennett (Manchester, N.H.: Sophia Institute Press, 2005).

After reading this book, and many of these authors' other great books, I realized that I am not crazy; I'm just wired in a unique way. Each of us has been programmed by God with a unique personality type, style, and energy level. What appeals to some may not appeal to others. Why? Because each of us is prewired with a certain personality type and temperament to fulfill the unique mission given to us by God Himself! This is an amazing book, and the Bennetts are gifted at knowing our human wiring and how this relates to our spiritual life.

Noise: How Our Media-Saturated Culture Dominates Lives and Dismantles Families, by Theresa Tomeo (West Chester, Pa.: Ascension Press, 2007).

As a former ad executive, I find *Noise* a great and easy read about the chaos and distractions that attack our lives today. My friend Theresa Tomeo lived in the tumultuous and cruel world of broadcast journalism and survived, by the grace of God, to share her findings with us.

The Church and New Media: Blogging Converts, Online Activists, and Bishops Who Tweet, by Brandon Vogt (Huntington, Ind.: Our Sunday Visitor, 2011).

Young Catholic blogger Brandon Vogt opens our eyes to the world of social media and other communication venues of the New Evangelization.

HOLY WISDOM

"For if I preach the gospel, that gives me no ground for boasting. For necessity is laid upon me. Woe to me if I do not preach the gospel!" (1 Corinthians 9:16)

POPE BENEDICT XVI
quotes from Paul's letter and argues for the urgency and necessity of evangelization. (address to the participants at the annual meeting of the Pontifical Mission Society, May 17, 2008).

The question confronting the Church today is not any longer whether the man in the street can grasp a religious message, but how to employ the communications media so as to let him have the full impact of the Gospel message.

POPE JOHN PAUL II
(*International Herald Tribune* [Paris], May 8, 1989)

The Church is missionary by nature and her principal task is evangelization, which aims to proclaim and to witness to Christ and to promote his Gospel of peace and love in every environment and culture.

POPE BENEDICT XVI
(address to the participants in the Fifth Annual Congress of Military Ordinariates, October 26, 2000)

Evangelization is in fact the grace and vocation proper to the Church, her deepest identity.

POPE PAUL VI
(*Evangelii Nuntiandi*, apostolic exhortation, December 8, 1975)

First let a little love find entrance into their hearts, and the rest will follow.

SAINT PHILIP NERI
(*Oratory of St. Philip Neri,* by H. Bowden, transcribed by Michael C. Tinkler, from the *Catholic Encyclopedia*, copyright © 1913 by the Encyclopedia Press, Inc.; electronic version copyright © 1996 by New Advent, Inc.)

Pray as though everything depended on God. Work as though everything depended on you.

SAINT AUGUSTINE
(quoted in Saint Ignatius of Loyola, *The Jesuits: Their Spiritual Doctrine and Practice*, p. 148)

The nation doesn't simply need what we have. It needs what we are.
SAINT TERESA BENEDICTA OF THE CROSS
(also known as Edith Stein) (Catholic Exchange, June 6, 2012)

Christ said, "I am the Truth"; he did not say "I am the custom."
SAINT TORIBIO
(from Rev. Alban Butler, *The Lives of the Fathers, Martyrs and Other Principal Saints*, vol. 3 [D. & J. Sadlier & Company, 1864])

As the family goes, so goes the nation and so goes the whole world in which we live.

POPE JOHN PAUL II
(homily given at Perth, Australia, November 30, 1986)

POWERFUL PRAYERS

Memorare

Remember, O most gracious Virgin Mary, that never was it known that any one who fled to thy protection, implored thy help, or sought thy intercession was left unaided. Inspired with this confidence, I fly unto thee, O Virgin of virgins, my Mother; to thee do I come; before thee I stand, sinful and sorrowful. O Mother of the Word Incarnate, despise not my petitions, but in thy mercy hear and answer me. Amen.

Hail Holy Queen

Hail, holy Queen, Mother of Mercy!
Our life, our sweetness, and our hope!
To thee do we cry, poor banished children of Eve;

to thee do we send up our sighs, mourning and weeping in
    this valley of tears.

Turn, then, most gracious Advocate, thine eyes of mercy
    toward us;

and after this our exile show unto us the blessed fruit of
    thy womb, Jesus.

O clement, O loving, O sweet Virgin Mary.

Pray for us O holy mother of God that we may be worthy
    of the promises of Christ.

The Guardian Angel Prayer

Angel of God, my guardian dear, to whom His love entrusts
me here, ever this day [night] be at my side, to light and
guard, to rule and guide. Amen.

Prayer to Saint Monica

Exemplary Mother of the great Augustine, you persever-
ingly pursued your wayward son, not with wild threats but
with prayerful cries to heaven.

    Intercede for all mothers in our day so that they may
learn to draw their children to God. Teach them how to
remain close to their children, even the prodigal sons and
daughters who have sadly gone astray. Amen.

    O glorious St. Monica, greatly challenged among moth-
ers, I feel particularly attracted by you who gave such an enlightened example of motherly love.

Who could understand better than you the anxieties and fears of a mother worrying about the eternal salvation of her children? You endured all, since in the order of nature, St. Augustine is the fruit of your womb, and in the order of grace, the fruit of your tears. For this reason I am greatly convinced that if you here on earth, with the sanctity of your life and the perseverance of your prayers, were one of the great models of the Christian mother, you must enjoy in heaven the privilege of being their singular protector.

Obtain for me the grace to faithfully imitate your virtues, and furthermore, may my children avoid those errors and failures you disapproved of so strongly in your son. And if it will happen, to my misfortune, that they too fall, grant me the grace to obtain with my prayers, supported by yours, as perfect a conversion as you were able to obtain for your son. Amen.

Prayer to Saint Michael

Saint Michael the Archangel,
defend us in battle;
be our protection against the wickedness and snares of the
    devil.
May God rebuke him, we humbly pray,
and do thou, O Prince of the heavenly host,
by the power of God,
thrust into hell Satan and all the evil spirits

who prowl about the world seeking the ruin of souls.
Amen.

Prayer of Saint Francis of Assisi

Lord, make me an instrument of your peace.
Where there is hatred, let me sow love;
where there is injury, pardon;
where there is doubt, faith;
where there is despair, hope;
where there is darkness, light;
and where there is sadness, joy.
O Divine Master, grant that I may not so much seek
to be consoled as to console;
to be understood as to understand;
to be loved as to love.
For it is in giving that we receive;
it is in pardoning that we are pardoned;
and it is in dying that we are born to eternal life. Amen.

Prayer to Saint Joseph

O St. Joseph, whose protection is so great, so strong, so prompt before the throne of God, I place in you all my interests and desires. O St. Joseph, do assist me by your powerful intercession and obtain for me from your Divine Son all spiritual blessings through Jesus Christ, our Lord;

so that having engaged here below your heavenly power, I may offer my thanksgiving and homage to the most loving of Fathers.

O St. Joseph, I never weary of contemplating you and Jesus asleep in your arms. I dare not approach while He reposes near your heart. Press Him in my name and kiss His fine head for me, and ask Him to return the kiss when I draw my dying breath. St. Joseph, patron of departing souls, pray for me. Amen.

Prayer to the Holy Spirit
(Attributed to Saint Catherine of Siena)

Holy Spirit, come into my heart; draw it to Thee by Thy power, O my God, and grant me charity with filial fear. Preserve me, O ineffable Love, from every evil thought; warm me, inflame me with Thy dear love, and every pain will seem light to me. My Father, my sweet Lord, help me in all my actions. Jesus, love, Jesus, love. Amen.

Prayer for the Gifts of the Holy Spirit
(Saint Alphonsus Liguori)

Holy Spirit, divine Consoler, I adore You as my true God, with God the Father and God the Son. I adore You and unite myself to the adoration You receive from the angels and saints.

I give You my heart and I offer my ardent thanksgiving for all the grace which You never cease to bestow on me.

O Giver of all supernatural gifts, who filled the soul of the Blessed Virgin Mary, Mother of God, with such immense favors, I beg You to visit me with Your grace and Your love and to grant me the gift of holy *fear*, so that it may act on me as a check to prevent me from falling back into my past sins, for which I beg pardon.

Grant me the gift of *piety*, so that I may serve You for the future with increased fervor, follow with more promptness Your holy inspirations, and observe your divine precepts with greater fidelity.

Grant me the gift of *knowledge*, so that I may know the things of God and, enlightened by Your holy teaching, may walk, without deviation, in the path of eternal salvation.

Grant me the gift of *fortitude*, so that I may overcome courageously all the assaults of the devil, and all the dangers of this world which threaten the salvation of my soul.

Grant me the gift of *counsel*, so that I may choose what is more conducive to my spiritual advancement and may discover the wiles and snares of the tempter.

Grant me the gift of *understanding*, so that I may apprehend the divine mysteries and by contemplation of heavenly things detach my thoughts and affections from the vain things of this miserable world.

Grant me the gift of *wisdom*, so that I may rightly direct all my actions, referring them to God as my last end; so

that, having loved Him and served Him in this life, I may have the happiness of possessing Him eternally in the next. Amen.

Come Holy Spirit

Come Holy Spirit, fill the hearts of Thy faithful and kindle in them the fire of Thy love.

V. Send forth Thy Spirit, and they shall be created;

R. And Thou shalt renew the face of the earth.

Let us pray.

O, God, who by the light of the Holy Spirit, did instruct the hearts of the faithful, grant that by the same Holy Spirit we may be truly wise and ever rejoice in His consolations. Through Christ our Lord. Amen.

Invocation to the Sacred Heart

(Saint Margaret Mary Alocoque)

O Heart of love, I put all my trust in Thee; for I fear all things from my own weakness, but I hope for all things from Thy goodness. Amen.

For the Help of the Sacred Heart

Take away, O my Jesus, the blindness of my heart, that I may know Thee; take away the hardness of my heart, that

I may fear Thee; take away the coldness of my heart, that I may resist everything that is contrary to Thy will; take away its heavy, earthly sluggishness and selfishness, that I may be capable of heroic sacrifice for Thy glory, and for the souls whom Thou has redeemed with Thy own most precious blood. Amen.

Prayer by Blessed John Henry Cardinal Newman
    (Prayed by Blessed Mother Teresa's Sisters of Charity)

Dear Jesus, help me to spread Your fragrance
    everywhere I go.
Flood my soul with Your spirit and life.
Penetrate and possess my whole being so utterly
that my life may only be a radiance of Yours.
Shine through me and be so in me
that every soul I come in contact with
may feel Your presence in my soul.
Let them look up and see no longer me, but only Jesus!
Stay with me and then I shall begin to shine as You shine,
so to shine as to be a light to others.
The light, O Jesus, will be all from You; none of it will
    be mine;
it will be you, shining on others through me.
Let me thus praise you in the way which you love best,
by shining on those around me.
Let me preach you without preaching, not by words
    but by example,

by the catching force, the sympathetic influence of what
    I do,
the evident fullness of the love my heart bears for you.
    Amen.

For the Peace of Christ
    (Blessed John Henry Cardinal Newman)

O most sacred, most loving heart of Jesus, Thou art concealed in the Holy Eucharist, and Thou beatest for us still. Now as then Thou sayest, "With desire I have desired." I worship Thee, then, with all my best love and awe, with my fervent affection, with my most subdued, most resolved will. O make my heart beat with Thy heart. Purify it of all that is earthly, all that is proud and sensual, all that is hard and cruel, of all perversity, of all disorder, of all deadness. So fill it with Thee, that neither the events of the day nor the circumstances of the time may have power to ruffle it; but that in Thy love and Thy fear it may have peace.

The shortest, simplest, and most powerful prayer: the name of *Jesus.*

CATHOLIC ORGANIZATIONS

I haven't traveled along my faith journey alone. Here's a list of great Catholic organizations that have blessed my life as well as the lives of many others:

CATHOLIC RADIO ASSOCIATION,
>
> a trade association for Catholic radio stations, www.catholicradioassociation.org

ETERNAL WORD TELEVISION NETWORK (EWTN),
>
> a Catholic television and radio network and website, www.ewtn.com

THE INTEGRATED CATHOLIC LIFE,
>
> an e-magazine about integrating faith, family, and world, www.integratedcatholiclife.org

KNIGHTS OF COLUMBUS,
>
> a Catholic fraternal benefits organization, www.kofc.org

KNIGHTS OF THE HOLY SEPULCHRE,
>
> the only lay institute of the Vatican State charged with providing for the needs of the Latin Patriarchate of Jerusalem; its members fund activities that support the Christian presence in the Holy Land, www.holysepulchre.net

LEGATUS,

>an organization of practicing Catholic lay men and women (along with their spouses) who are CEOs, presidents, managing partners, and business owners who live and share the Catholic faith in every area of their lives, www.legatus.org

MARIAN CONFERENCE,

>an organization that hosts conferences across the United States, promoting devotion to our Blessed Mother and helping participants grow closer to Christ, www.marianconference.org

OPUS DEI,

>a personal prelature whose members strive to turn work and daily activities into occasions for growing closer to God, serving others, and improving society, www.opusdei.org

ORDER OF MALTA,

>an organization whose members make a commitment to achieve spiritual perfection while serving the poor and the sick, www.orderofmalta.int

Acknowledgments

None of the fruit coming from this book, our apostolates, or my life would be possible without the merciful love and guidance of Jesus and His Church! I am so thankful for the grace from the Holy Trinity, our Blessed Mother's love, and the choirs of heaven who are praying for this mission of the New Evangelization. It is with sincere love and gratitude that I dedicate this book to my beloved wife, Tricia, along with our incredible daughters, Katie, Kimberly, and Tina, for a lifetime of support, prayers, encouragement, patience, and love! You have helped me grow as a Christian husband and father, and provided essential ingredients for our apostolic mission. To my parents, Byron and Jackie Peterson; my grandparents; son-in-law Raymond; and my sister Cindy and her family who also helped nurture the growth of my Catholic faith, I am also so grateful to all of you. Finally, I dedicate this book to the countless souls who are on their journey home to Jesus and His Church.

I own a debt of gratitude to Dr. Scott W. Hahn, who encouraged me to start this book and generously wrote the Foreword. Thank you to Patrick Madrid and the encouragement of our many other inspirational Boards of Advisors, the incredible dedication of Frank Dibugnara and Bob Trussell, and the spiritual direction and friendship of Fr. Doug Lorig, Deacon Joe Lessard, Brendan Case, Joe Stark, and Bishop Sam Jacobs. Additionally, I am sincerely honored to serve our Lord in His work of the New Evangelization alongside my colleagues at Catholics Come Home and VirtueMedia. Thank you to Ms. Bobbi Friedrich for her inspiration in 1997, along with our countless supporters, prayer partners, bishops, priests, and coworkers at various dioceses, respect life ministries, and Legatus chapters across the U.S. and abroad. For you my brothers and sisters in Christ, my deepest appreciation and respect.

To Gary Jansen, my editor at Random House/ Image Publishing, thank you for your expert mentoring and patience with me as a growing author.